Television Advertising Ethics and Human Rights

Television Advertising Ethics and Human Rights

Juhi P. Pathak

SHIPRA

₹ 1500; US$ 60

ISBN: 978-93-86262-71-4

First Published in India in 2018

Television Advertising Ethics and Human Rights

Published by:
SHIPRA PUBLICATIONS
LG 18-19, Pankaj Central Market
I.P. Ext., Patparganj, Delhi 110092, India
+91 11 2223 5152/6152; 96500 28065
info@shiprapublication.com
www.shiprapublication.com

Preface

The book deals with the various aspects of human rights and how they have been portrayed by the Indian television advertising media. It reflects both the positive and negative portrayals of important issues relating to human rights concentrating on areas of child rights, privacy of women, portrayal of lasciviousness, colour discrimination as well as peace and communal harmony.

The subject of the use of infants and children in advertising is becoming a major concern in developing and developed countries. There are many organizations, government and private, that have compared children working in advertisements with child labour.

The world of advertising uses babies to peddle products related to them, but the point is – will the product sell more if the baby is shown unclad? The second pertinent question is – are those babies being used by the parents for monetary or for glamour gains? The third point is that just like many of us are ashamed to show our unclad infant photographs in albums to guests visiting our house, those visuals of the baby sitting in a puddle of toilet as shown in the advertisements, can be a reason of its embarrassment when s/he grows up. An in-depth study is made to see if using clippings of unclad babies will violate their rights of privacy and other related rights.

This work also takes into consideration the psychological aspect of the babies in this regard after they grow up. It studies the current advertising codes of conduct and whether the above given angles are being taken into account by them. Various International Conventions and the laws of our land regarding Child Rights have also been taken into consideration and studies the provisions for the protection of human rights of the child in this context.

Pregnancy and child birth are a matter of great happiness for any woman; but, at the same time, it is a matter that concerns her privacy too. But, it has been observed that there is a recent trend in the field of Indian advertising where child birth has been trivialized to cash in profits by the private players. The showing of child delivery in a derogatory manner is indeed an infringement on the right to privacy of a woman. This study highlights the cases that have been on trend in the present scenario of advertising in India; and evaluate as to what extent the privacy of a woman is hampered through such portrayal. And recent laws prevalent in our country to curtail such violation of the right to privacy of woman.

Advertisement is the process of communicating the most persuasive selling message possible, to the right potential consumer of products or services at the right time and place, at the least possible cost. Advertisement acts as a bridge between the potential seller and the buyer. Advertising is a pervasive, powerful force that shapes the attitudes and behaviour of the present society. The modern market economy has also seen a boom in the advertising industry. In order to beat the competitors in the highly competitive and fast market; combined with the motive of grabbing eyeballs in an instant and getting talked about at large even for not-so-good reasons, at times, advertisers go beyond the traditional role of 'fair and truthful' information and portray obscene, undesirable and unethical scenes that have a detrimental effect on the society.

The work elaborates instances of colour discrimination; and thereby the violation of advertising ethics in context to Indian television. It also highlights the laws and codes that are already in place; but their lack of implementation; and specifically, the lack of awareness on the part of the viewers have made the scene worse. It concludes with effective suggestions through which the problem of colour discrimination through television advertisements can be dealt with in an efficient way.

India is the birthplace of several religions – Hinduism, Buddhism, Jainism, and Sikhism, and is a home since thousands of years to communities like Jewish, Zoroastrians, Muslims, and Christians. The vast majority of citizens of all religious groups live in peaceful coexistence and are conscious of religious freedom and minority rights; however, at times, violence between religious groups do occur. Advertisers have always shirked away from incorporating the concept of 'religion' in the television commercials (TVCs). But, lately we see a trend wherein the companies and advertisers have roped in the concept of 'religious harmony' to promote their products. The examples of such TVCs being that of 'Kaun Banega Crorepati', 'Brooke Bond Red Label' and 'HavellsHiMu'. These three advertisements are being aired on national television and it is felt that such portrayal can go a long way in bridging the differences between the various religious communities. The study analyzes the recent laws prevalent in our country to promote harmony among various religious groups.

The intermittent wars and conflicts lead to human rights violations. In this context, the work also analyzes the positive role of television advertisements in portraying the Indo-Pak relations from an Indian perspective. Advertisements featuring gay rights have also been circulating in print, television and internet. India is among countries with a social element of a third gender. But mental, physical, emotional and economic violence against LGBT community in India prevails.

This work seeks to understand the role of such television advertisements in analysing the status of LGBT rights in India in context of the Human Rights angle. Thus, the entire volume deals with the various television advertisements and their portrayal with reference to the important issues relating to human rights.

Dr. Juhi P. Pathak

Acknowledgements

I begin by expressing my sincere thanks to Dr. Chandan Kumar Goswami, former Head, Department of Communication and Journalism, Gauhati University. It was Mr. Goswami who introduced me to my Co-Guide, Prof. Dr. Kandarpa Das; and as such, I am ever grateful to him. Mr. Goswami, with his unending treasure of motivating talks, have had always made sure that I do not deviate from my goal in life. It was he who took care that I always felt at home in the Department that I had just joined in the year 2013.

I also express my gratefulness to Prof. Dr. Kandarpa Das who further introduced me to my mentor – an icon in the Assamese society – Dr. Sitanath Lahkar; and together they left no stones unturned to see that my work finishes on time and, that too, without any possible flaws.

The success of my first book, 'Introduction to Media Laws and Ethics' (2014) which helped me to earn the title of 'World's Youngest Textbook Author in the Legal subject' provided me immense confidence to work on media laws and study its connection with human rights. I extend my gratefulness to Mr. D Kumar, Shipra Publications who had the faith that a then '24 year old' can write on such an important topic.

I convey my respect and gratefulness to the current Head of the Department, Dr. Ankuran Dutta about whom I had always heard but had very little chances to interact with. However, whenever I spoke to him; he had always instilled positivity and motivation in me through his measured words. I am grateful to my seniors, friends, colleagues and the staff at the Department and everyone else who had motivated me. I also extend my gratefulness to my teachers for providing me with the best of knowledge in my subject and my friends, especially Mr. Pranesh Kumar Roy, Ms. Mrinal Singh and Mr. Abhishek Choudhary, along with their families, who have always inspired me to achieve my goals.

I thank my paternal grandmother, Late Mrs. Abala Pathak who always inquired and looked forward to see me complete my research. It is with her blessings along with the blessings of my ancestors that included educationists like Late Benudhar Rajkhowa, Late Anangadhar Rajkhowa and Late Brahmananda Pathak that today I have reached this stage in life. I take this opportunity to convey my deepest respect and gratitude to my parents, Mr. Pranab Pathak and Mrs. Tandrali Pathak along with my sister Ms. Hridisthita Pathak for their constant and untiring support throughout my life.

Above all, I humbly acknowledge the presence of the Almighty whose blessings and grace have always been with me.

Dr. Juhi P. Pathak

Contents

Annexures

1

Concept and History of Advertising

Meaning

The term advertising is derived from the Latin word, '*advertere*' which means to turn attention towards a specific thing.[1] Advertising simply means a public announcement. But, nowadays, the functions of advertisements go beyond announcements as they persuade the prospective buyer, remind the existing buyers, create demand, brand preference and brand loyalty; apart from neutralising the effects of the advertisements of the competitors.

Advertising is aimed at a group of persons and not an individual. These groups of persons are not the general public; but the target audience who are also the potential customers. In advertising, unlike personal selling, immediate feedback cannot be taken. Thus, it is a paid form of non-personal way of communication with a group of target audience through mass media like television, newspapers, magazines, radio, internet et al.

Definitions

American Marketing Association: Advertising is a paid form of non-personal presentation and promotion of goods, services or ideas by an identified sponsor.[2]

Philip Kotler: Advertising is a non-personal form of communication conducted through paid media under clear sponsorship.[3]

John J. Myers: Advertising is dissemination of information concerning an idea, service or product to compel action in accordance with the interest of the advertiser.[4]

John Kennedy: Advertising is the substitute of human salesman.[5]

David Ogilvy: Advertising means to develop favourable brand image to enlarge market share and to increase the profits of the organisation in the long run.[6]

Features of Advertising

1. *Paid form*: Advertising is never free of cost. The company issuing an advertisement has to pay the media. The scale of payment depends on media-circulation, type of media and media-popularity. Advertisements appear in newspapers, radio and television because the advertisers have purchased the space or time to communicate information to the target audience or, in other words, prospective customers.
2. *Non-personal:* Advertising has no face to face contact with the buyers; and as such it is called non-personal salesmanship. Here, the message is transmitted to the target audience with the help of mass media like newspapers, magazines, radio, television or internet; and not through direct inter-personal communication.
3. *Promotion of ideas*: Advertising is not only the promotion of goods and services, but also of ideas.
4. *Identified sponsor*: Advertising is done by an identified sponsor. The sponsor could be the producer or the trader. The identity of the sponsor is mentioned in the advertisement. This indicates that the advertisement attributes the source for the ideas and opinion it presents.
5. *Influence buyer's behaviour*: Advertisements influence the attitudes and behaviour of the buyers in favour of the advertised products or services.
6. *Element of marketing mix*: The four major elements of marketing mix are product, promotion, price and place. Advertising is an important part of 'promotion'. Without proper promotion, other elements of the marketing mix cannot achieve their desired objectives.
7. *Promotion mix:* Advertising is one of the four elements of promotion mix; the other three being personal selling, sales promotion and publicity. It is the most cost-effective method of promotion as it creates demand, stimulates sales and reaches the target audience quickly and effectively.

Advertising Scenario in India

Mukesh and Ranju Trehan in their book, '*Advertising and Sales Management*' have very aptly elucidated the advertising scenario in India.[3] Nowadays, producing the goods is easier than satisfying and attracting consumers. Many brands are available for almost every product in the market. Every company wants to increase its market share. Advertisers make a lot of effort to attract and persuade the prospective customers to purchase their products and services. Advertising has been recognised as an important tool of promotion; thereby making it a cost-effective tool of mass communication. Evidence of increasing importance of advertising is clearly reflected from the increase in advertising expenditure. Today, both the quality and quantity of advertisements have increased as we are exposed to so many of them than at any point of time in the past. At present, the advertising industry ranks 5th amongst the big industries of the world; the first four industries being oil, automobiles, computers and electronics.[3] The growth in both traditional and newer media has contributed significantly to the growth of advertising. Advertising industry has become very competitive; thus, making advertising a very respectable profession. The advertising industry in India has recorded a significant growth. Advertising spending which were just about Rs 49 crores in the year 1961, have increased to about Rs. 10,050 crores in the year 2001. In India advertising business is growing at the rate of about 35 percent per annum. But still, per capita spending on advertising is far below as compared to developed countries. Per capita advertising expenditure in India is merely $9 against about $80 in Singapore.

Main aspects of Advertising Scene in India

Advertising scene in India can be summed up under the following headings:

1. ***Increase in advertising spending:*** According to data available from 1961 to 2017, it has been noticed that advertising spending has recorded a significant growth in India. This is clear from the following table.

Year	*Advertising spending (Rs in crores)*
1961	49[3]
1971	65[3]
1981	472[3]
1991	1545[3]
2001	10,050[3]
2011	27433[7]
2012	28854[7]
2013	32106[7]
2014	37405[7]
2015	49759[8]
2016	55672[7]
2017	61204[7] (Projected)

The total advertising expenditure in India was merely Rs 49 crores in the year 1961 and this spending rose to Rs 55672 crores in the year 2016. GroupM, the leading global media management investment conglomerate, on 14 February 2017, released its biannual advertising expenditure report forecasting India's advertising investment to reach an estimated Rs. 61,204 crores in 2017. This represents a growth of 10% for the calendar year 2017 over the corresponding period in 2016. Spending on advertisement in India is increasing at the rate of about 35 per cent per annum.[3]

2. ***Growth in media:*** All forms of Indian media have registered an impressive increase during the last few years. Internet has emerged as a media of the new millennium. With the growth rate in literacy in India, the number of readers of newspapers and magazines have registered a significant growth. With the increase in income levels and increase in television channels, the number of television viewers have increased significantly. Television, now, is recognised as the most powerful advertising media in India. The growth in cable television has created opportunity for small advertisers. Now, small advertisers can afford cable television advertisements to be shown in their local regions. With the growth in personal computers, internet advertising is also on the rise. At present media is facing the problem of clutter, that is, too much of advertising on the media.
3. ***Growth of advertising agencies:*** The growth of advertising agencies has been accepted world-wide. Now-a-days, dependence on advertising agencies is increasing very fast. The number of ad-agencies in India has increased from 14 in the year 1939 to 862 (as registered with Indian Newspapers Society as of June 7, 2017). Many advertising agencies operating in India are now foreign-owned.
4. ***Legal regulations in advertising*:** The government has passed various laws to regulate advertising and to protect the interest of the consumers in India. The main aim of these regulations is to check untruthful and misleading advertisements. (Refer Annexure - IV for the list of laws, rules and regulations that deal with advertisements.)
5. ***Professional bodies*:** There are three professional bodies relating to advertising: i.e. the advertiser, the advertising agency and the media of advertising. The Indian Society of Advertisers (ISA) is the representative body of advertisers. The Advertising Agencies Association of India (AAAI) represents advertising agencies. The Indian Newspaper Society (INS) is the representative organisation of

newspapers and magazines and the Indian Broadcasting Society (IBS) represents the broadcasting companies. Similarly Advertising Club of India, Advertising Standards Council of India etc. are also working as professional bodies in the area of advertising. These organisations and associations protect the interest and dignity of advertisers, media owners, ad agencies and consumers at large.

6. ***Increase in market coverage*:** Earlier advertising focussed only on the richer sections of the society, but now the area of advertising has expanded. Presently, it covers all the sections of the society viz. rich consumer group, middle class consumer group, poor consumer group, urban and rural consumer groups. Now, advertisers develop advertisements keeping in view the religious and cultural diversities, differences in lifestyle, income level, sex ratio, education level, differences in consumption pattern etc. Similarly, different advertisements are designed for attracting the attention of different age groups. Thus, advertising today focuses on all segments of the market.
7. ***Increasing trend of branded products*:** The earlier Indian market was flooded with various unbranded and local products. But now the trend is towards branded products. The scope of advertising has increased with the increase in literacy rate, awareness and standard of living of the Indian people; thus a major section of people today have become brand-conscious.
8. ***Advertising of goods as well as of services:*** Earlier advertisements focussed on physical goods; but now advertising of services is also very common. For example, advertisements of insurance companies, banking companies, tele-communication companies, tour and travel agencies, courier services, entertainment industries etc. are often seen in media.
9. ***Increasing non-commercial and classified advertising*:** Earlier advertisements were issued mainly for commercial purposes. But, now non-commercial advertisements are also becoming very popular in India. Various social organisations, government bodies, political organisations today are seen issuing advertisements. For example, advertisements on awareness about various social issues and social problems like AIDS, female foeticide, drug addiction, girl-education etc. We also see advertisements that issue public notifications like the last date for filing income-tax return, date for pulse polio drops etc. Similarly classified advertisements under specific headings are very common, for example, property for sale, tender notice, vehicles for sale, matrimonial, public appointments etc.

Origin and Growth of Advertising

Dr. Shaila Bootwala, Dr. M.D. Lawrence and Prof. Sanjay R. Mali in their book, *'Advertising and sales management'* illustrates the history of advertising. They illustrate seven stages to study the progress of advertising over the centuries.[1]

1. *Ancient time – fifth century*: Advertising as we know today, was not used till about two centuries ago. It has the longest history taking us back to the history of mankind and human civilisation. Advertising began with the discovery of the art of communication; with the earliest tool probably being the word of mouth. The use of advertising as a medium to transmit information dates as back as ancient Rome and Greece. Before the development of printing, signs and criers were used to disseminate information about goods or services; and also to impress their customers of the quality of their products. Merchants had symbols that told of their trade. Thus, a shop sign as a means for identifying the place of business is a relic of this time.
2. *The Dark Age*: 'The Dark Age' (465 AD to 800 AD) starts with the downfall of the Roman empire and the rule of Charlemagne. Trade suffered a setback during the fall of the Roman empire; thereby diminishing the commerce and trade routes. Not much about advertising is heard in this period. But that does not mean that advertising was not in use entirely. Public barkers equipped with horns and bells, hand executed signs and placards were used to attract the attention of the potential customers.
3. *Thirteenth century*: During this age, advertising signs gained maximum use. Criers for the taverns were so numerous in Paris in this century that they formed a union and were chartered by King Philip Augustus. The giving of free samples started during this era by these criers.
4. *Fifteenth century*: In the year 1438 Johann Gutenberg invented the casting moveable type and printed the Bible in 1456. This discovery in the west is the first leap in the field of advertising. New methods of advertising, like printed posters, handbills and pamphlets, were then made available.
5. *Sixteenth and seventeenth century*: This was the time when the techniques of printing evolved and larger number of newspapers were introduced; although some of them were like newsletters. The early advertisements in these newspapers were more like announcements made by the importers of new products in England; for example

advertisements of coffee (1652), Chocolates (1657) and tea (1658) were introduced through newspaper advertisements. The earlier advertisements in the newspapers were for books and marriage offers. Initially, advertisement in newspapers was that of 'pioneering advertising' in nature. England saw the face of competitive advertising much later in 18th century.

6. *Eighteenth and nineteenth century*: This period witnessed the birth and blossoming of competitive advertising. Around the year 1840, several newspapers were selling space in New York. The age old principle of '*Caveat Emptor*' (the principle that the buyer should check the quality of goods before buying) ruled the transactions. Nineteenth century was marked with the introduction of the concept of 'brand advertising'. This is the period when 'point of purchase' advertising became popular.
7. *Twentieth century*: The twentieth century saw the discovery of the radio, television and satellite communication. The world had become a global village; thereby giving an immense boost to the advertising sector. Advertising can be viewed and heard across the length and breadth of the world. Information technology and mass communication has developed to such an extent that no business can run without advertising. The success and failure of a business largely depends on its advertising strategy.

Thus, the advertising industry that started with barkers eventually culminated into a very powerful mass media of communication. It is an industry at the very core of all businesses; and something without which no business can exist today.

Another classification of the history of advertising states that it might be divided into six periods or stages as follows:[4]

1. *Pre-printing period*: In this period (prior to the fifteenth century) the town criers were means of advertising. The government provided them with charters and the organised themselves in a sort of union.
2. *Early printing period*: This was the period (from the fifteenth century to about 1840) when the printing press was invented and there was a renaissance of learning; and the combination meant much to advertising business as it had led to the large scale production of advertisements for wide distribution.
3. *Period of expansion*: United States witnessed vast changes in the advertising business in this period (from 1840 to 1900). The newspaper publishers and printers handled the advertising by selling space to procure money for their growth and survival.

4. *Period of consolidation from 1900 to 1925:* United States saw a protest for misleading and untruthful advertising in 1911. The Curtis Publishing Company, Printers, Ink. Inc and other companies led the fight. Advertising world witnessed a remarkable development in the year 1920 with the advent of radio.
5. *Period of scientific development*: The period (from 1925 to 1945) witnessed the application of scientific methods in resolving advertising related problems. Observation, recording and classification of facts started to begin through scientific devices for testing the strategies for sales effectiveness. This dependence on science substituted the philosophical yardstick of performance with a more scientific one.
6. *Period of business and social integration*: This period (post war from 1945 to the present) witnessed prosperity and development in the advertising industry; which was further boosted in 1950s with the invention of television.

The growth and popularity of the television medium brought about revolutionary changes in the advertising industry.

Om Gupta, in the book, '*Advertising in India: Trends and impact*' classified the history of advertising into two types: Prior to industrialization and Post industrialization.[5]

1. Prior to Industrialisation

Om Gupta writes that advertising is dated back to Christian era. One of the first known methods of advertising was outdoor signs that would be painted on the wall of a building and were usually very eye-catching.

Ancient Egyptians and Greeks sensed the benefits of product promotion. Archaeologists have found 'signs' in the ruins of ancient Rome and Pompeii. Others claim that prehistoric cave paintings were a form of advertising. But it is true that advertising has been around for as long as there had been goods to sell and a medium to promote them – from the crier in the street to the handbill tacked on the tree.

Advertising as we know today began during the last quarter of the nineteenth century. Advertising agencies were relatively unknown then and, those that existed, had ill-defined responsibilities.

During the past century, large American manufacturers have played an important role in developing the profession of advertising. But in earlier years, it was United Kingdom that took the leadership in terms and creativity.

In the United Kingdom, the first advertising agent was probably one William Taylor, who opened an office in London's Warwick Square in the year 1786. The firm was later known as Taylor & Newton; and it acted as an advertising sales representative for printers – several of whom had launched newspapers to promote their trade.

Advertising was a well established practice in the late colonial and early democratic periods in America, but these advertisements were neither as appealing to the eye nor as cleverly crafted as were their counterparts in England. The type was so illegible that Benjamin Franklin once observed: "If you ever have any secrets that you wish to be well kept, get them printed in the papers."[5]

Moreover, the United States was a predominantly rural nation. With a sparse, predominantly rural population, and without an efficient system of transportation and communication, the country had neither the need for nor the means of concerned national advertising campaigns. Historian Lewin Antherton observed that "in general, the early advertising was dreary, matter of fact reading, served a limited purpose and was completely devoid of... customer appeal...one advertisement was like all others."[5] Advertising took a leap forward, of course, with the appearance of the printing press and movable type- an invention credited to German Johaness Gutenberg in the year 1447.

S. H. H. Kazmi and Satish K Batra, in their book, '*Advertising And Sales Promotion*' writes that it was only after nearly forty years of the invention of the movable type that the first known printed advertisement in English language appeared. William Caxton of London printed the first advertisement; which was a handbill of rules that was put on the Church doors for the guidance of the clergy at Easter.[6]

The first advertisement in any language to be printed on a circulated sheet appeared in a German news pamphlet in about 1525. It was an advertisement that advocated the virtues of a mysterious drug.

The first printed newspaper in England– 'The Weekly News of London' came out in 1622; but, it was only in 1625, that the first advertisement was printed in one of the English newspapers.

The first printed advertisement – about a reward for the capture of a thief – appeared in 1704 in America in the 'Boston Newsletter'.

By the middle of 17th century, advertisements in the form of announcements appeared in England's weekly newspapers that were called 'Mercuries'. The first of coffee advertisements appeared in 1652, followed by chocolate in 1657 and tea in 1658.

There were advances in American advertising in the larger cities during the 1820s and 1830s with improvements in the printing technology and a change in advertising philosophy.

James Gordon Bennett, Sr., the 'New York Herald' and other New York penny press newspapers prided themselves on speaking directly to mass public in understandable and accessible terms, and they wanted their advertising to have the same appeal.

In 1848, Bennett began changing the Herald's advertising every day, turning them into news, just like the editorial matter. The precursors of advertising agencies also date from this period.

By the 1840s, Volney B. Palmer was listing his 'coal and advertising' agency in New York City's Business Directory. The very description of the business – 'Coal and advertising' – illustrates how undifferentiated advertising was in those days.

Maurice J Mandell, in the book '*Advertising*' writes that Palmer was the first advertising agent who established an office in Philadelphia. For a fee, he worked as an agent for newspapers. He sold space to advertisers; and helped them in media selection. He did not provide any creative or planning services to the clients.[9]

Modern advertising really began in the 1880s, when new methods of manufacturing led to greatly increased output and decreased costs for the producers of consumer goods.

Prior to the 1880s, the American marketing system had been characterised by an intricate set of wholesalers, jobbers and other middlemen whose most important function was to buy in large lots and sell in smaller ones. In this age, the wholesaler was the king but, in the new era of 1880s, the importance of the packaged goods manufacturer greatly increased. What manufacturers could package in their own plant, they could brand. What they could brand, they could advertise. What they could distribute nationally, they could advertise nationally.

Daniel A. Pope has written, "This necessitated the growth of advertising agencies and dictated their activities" and also "tipped the balance in advertising from information to persuation."[7]

John E. Powers, in the late 1880s, emerged as a great copywriter. His approach was – no catchy headlines, no brag, no pressure. J. Walter Thompson, a young advertising Executive at that time but, destined to become the inventor of modern advertising agency, signed an exclusive contract with twenty-five best American magazines; and had an impressive list of advertisers. Albert Lasker (father of modern advertising) and Claude C. Hopkins got together in the last decade of the 19th century and introduced the inclusion of 'record of results' in professional advertising business and 'reason why' approach to advertising copy respectively.

Later the 'reason why' approach of Hopkins was challenged by Theodore F. McManus of General Motors. McManus believed in producing impressionistic copy by incorporating original art, creative layouts and elegant writing to create a positive image of the company and its products.

The list of achievements in the field of advertising in the nineteenth century would be incomplete if we do not mention the advertising agency – Lord and Thomas. John N. Ingham, in the book, '*Biographical Dictionary of American Business Leaders*' writes that the agency had been founded by Daniel M. Lord and Ambrose L. Thomas in 1872 and in 1898 had $800,000 billings. The firm had two remarkable copywriters – Claude C. Hopkins and John E. Kennedy.[10] Hopkins was particularly good at understanding the consumer and how advertising should be integrated in the total marketing effort. Kennedy was known to have believed that advertising was 'salesmanship in print'; and tried to provide a reason why customers should buy the advertised products.

John McDonough and Karen Egolf, in their book, '*The Advertising Age Encyclopedia of Advertising*' writes that Lord and Thomas, under the influence of Kennedy, was also responsible for introducing the 'Hard-Sell' strategy in advertising; a concept later copied by numerous other advertising agencies. Lord and Thomas was also the pioneer in developing the concept of 'brand images'.[11]

National advertisers provided the media and advertising agencies with a new set of clients whose standards of conduct were far higher than those preceding them. The most widely advertised consumer products through most of the nineteenth century had been patent medicines for which their advertisers made extravagantly false claims. As late as 1893, according to Pope, more than half of sample of over a hundred firms, spending more than fifty thousand dollars annually on advertising, were patent medicine manufacturers, whose advertisements were often of the 'cancer cure' variety.[9] But the new companies depended upon repeated purchase behaviour and thus, to build a bond of trust with the consumer, they had to eschew blatant falsehoods.

For the consumer product market, advertising became the marketing analogy to assembly-line production techniques. It was systematised mass salesmanship, which became a key weapon in the arsenal of companies seeking to create and build brands.

With the new mix of advertising, clients and the new conception of advertising came a host of changes in the trade that sharply differentiated the 20th century practice from the previous era. Among the most important changes were those in the areas of copywriting, research and source of compensation.

Through most of the nineteenth century, the principal function of the nation's advertising agencies was to buy space in publications at wholesale rate and sell it to advertisers at retail. In 1892, the 'N.W. Ayer and Son Agency' in Philadelphia hired its first full-time copywriter to write the advertisement itself.

Soon after, Albert Davis Lasker of the Chicago agency of 'Lord and Thomas' greatly boosted the prestige of the copywriting function within the agency. He founded the 'reason why' school, which held that an advertising had to give the customer a specific reason (perhaps the most accurate description would be 'rational sounding excuse') to purchase a product. This approach contrasted with the bulk of previous copy, which had often consisted of an announcement accompanied by disconnected and incredible claims to excellence.

Modern business corporations and advertising agencies make a major effort to research the projected and actual impact of their advertising. Research at agencies dates back to 1879, when Ayer undertook its first such project.

Since then agencies, their clients and independent market research firms- often assisted by marketing academicians and economists- have spent large sums to determine advertising's effectiveness.

Advertising agencies have always been intermediaries between advertisers and the mass media. During much of the nineteenth century, it was unclear whom the agency represented. Was it primarily a seller of media space or a seller of a manufacturer's product? In the twentieth century, the answer had been the latter. Agencies sell products by buying space or time and compensated by manufacturers.

The most visible change in advertising in the past hundred years has resulted from the new technology of broadcasting.

Initially, many thought that advertising over the 'ether' would never be accepted by the public because it would constitute an obnoxious intrusion into the home of the owner of the radio set. And even if it did not prove unacceptable on grounds of taste, many felt that radio advertising should be prohibited as a matter of public policy.

Herbert Hoover, when he was Secretary of Commerce, said at a conference on Radio in 1922 that it was inconceivable that we should allow so great a possibility for service to be drowned in advertising chatter.

By the end of the decade, however, advertisers and their agents had come to realise radio's possibilities. With its drama and immediacy, radio could convey their message directly to the consumer who would not need to purchase a publication or even be literate.

2. Post-Industrialisation

Advertising got into its stride with the Industrial Revolution – aided and abetted by the rise of the newspapers as a mass medium. Advances in technology meant consumer goods could be produced and packaged on a previously un-dreamed of scale. This encouraged local manufacturers to seek far flung new markets. In order to etch the names and virtues of their products into memories of the target customers, they branded their goods – and thus the concept of 'brand advertising' started.

In Britain, one of the most prominent clients of the day was 'A&F Pears', makers of Pears' soap. The company's success was assured by Thomas J. Barrett who joined the firm in 1862. He successfully secured one of the first celebrity endorsements from actress Lillie Langtry and also convinced the popular artist Sir John Everett Millais to sell him a painting of a young boy gazing at rising soap bubbles. He further persuaded Millais to add a bar of Pears' soap to the scene. Thus, quite easily 'bubbles' became one of the earliest advertising icons, and set the tone for a highly successful campaign.

In his book, '*A complete guide to advertising* (1984)', Torin Douglas[12] recounts: 'Firms such as 'Cadbury and Fry' started packaging their products, not simply to protect them and preserve their quality, but also to establish their quality by the use of the company's own name. Instead of leaving it to the retailer to determine which company's product a customer would buy, they began to build their own relationship with the customers.'

Douglas highlights two other crucial factors in the rise of British advertising. 'The Education Act of 1870 in Britain provided elementary education for all, and this, combined with the abolition of tax on newspapers that had taken place 15 years before, led to a huge increase in the numbers of newspapers produced and sold. For the first time, advertisers had a mass-circulation press in which to promote their goods.'[10]

History of Television Advertising

The United States witnessed an exceptional degree of commercialisation of television in 1950s. Because of their access to more air-time, the American advertisers could promote commercial messages to wide market segments (including children). Through television, advertisers get their products endorsed by celebrities along with a clear demonstration of the same.

Norman J. Medoff and Barbara Kaye in their book, '*Electronic Media: Then, Now, and Later*' writes that the public got its first glimpse of television at the 1939 New York World Fair but the World War II interrupted television set production and programme transmission; stalling television's adoption by consumers until three years after the war. In 1948 the economy was booming and American consumers became very enthusiastic about television.[13]

At first, television advertising was based largely on radio's sponsorship model. Advertisers and their agencies produced sponsored programmes. However, television programmes were much more expensive than radio programmes; and agencies and advertisers found themselves spending thousands of dollars each week. 'The Kudner Agency' spent about $8000 per week for 'Texaco Star Theatre' (1948-53) and 'Frigidaire' spent about $100,000 for each 'Bob Hope' special it sponsored. The high cost of television sponsorship kept all; but a few, of the largest advertisers off the air. It soon became apparent that the model for television advertising had to change.

NBC television Executive Pat Weaver extended William Paley's idea of selling ad time within radio programmes to television; and came up with what is called as magazine style of television advertising; also known as spot or participation advertising. Weaver realised that television could make more money by selling time within and between programmes to several sponsors than relying on only one sponsor to bear the entire cost. His idea was similar to placement of advertisements between magazine articles. With Weaver's plan, advertisers found it more convenient to buy one-minute spots than the entire 15 or 30 minutes programme. Affordable airtime brought even the lesser known advertisers to television for the first time; and brought a revolution in the television advertising industry.

'The Bulova Watch Company' was the first advertiser to venture to television. On July 1, 1941 'Bulova' paid $9 to a New York City television station for a 20 second ad that aired during a baseball game.

Throughout the 1960s, most television commercials were sold in 60-seconds units known as 'spots'. Spots brought in tough competition among advertisers as they were struggling for the audience's attention. As such they had to come up with creative ways to make their products and brands stand out from the others. Slogans, jingles and catchy phrases thus made their way into the commercials.

Television advertising took a new turn in 1971 after the US Federal Government banned commercials featuring tobacco products. Cigarette companies had been among television's largest advertisers; but, the ban had left broadcasters scrambling to fill unsold ad time. Television networks realised that there were companies who could not buy airtime in 60-seconds block; but were willing to buy 30-seconds units. This arrangement was profitable for the television networks as well as they could earn more money through two 30-seconds slots than one 60-seconds one.

Norman J. Medoff and Barbara Kaye in their book, '*Electronic Media: Then, Now, and Later*' also writes about the gradual variation in television advertisement spots. In 1965, about 70% of all commercials were 60 seconds in length. Four years after the 1971 ban on tobacco commercials, only 11% of commercials were of 60 seconds and the rest were 30-seconds spots. By 1985, almost 90% were of 30-seconds spots. Throughout the 1980s, the length of commercials began to vary from 10, 15, 20 and 45 seconds spots. The 15-seconds spots gradually got the fascination of the advertisers and by 1990s they accounted for one-third of all commercials and by 2008 about four out of ten spots were of 15-seconds in length. Although very rare, but, sponsorship advertisements still occur. For example, the 'Ford Motor Company' was the sole sponsor of the movie 'Schindler's List' when it made its television debut in 1997 and in the early 2000s, 'Kleenex' sponsored movies such as 'An Officer And A Gentleman' and 'Steel Magnolias'.[11]

History of Advertising in India

Kruti Shah and Alan D'Souza, in their book, '*Advertising and promotion*', gave a detailed analysis of the history of advertising in India. The primitive history of advertising can be dated back to the beginning of civilisation with word of mouth advertising by hawkers. Harappa and Mohenjo-Daro indicated names, similar to present day trademarks, engraved on excavated metal, stone or earthen wares. Thus, wall paintings or stone engravings indicate an early tool for advertising.

Religious propagation was probably the earliest objective for advertising. Emperor Ashoka, between 563 and 232 B.C, had set up pillar and rock edicts (form of outdoor advertising) to spread the messages of Buddha. The paintings in the Ajanta, Amravati and Sanchi cave temples can be compared to indoor visual communication.

Until the advent of British rule in India, advertising was not a business agenda. The reasons were that India was the unique example of domestic commercial activities. India was in 'Village Economy' stage in the pre-British era where the relations between the producers and consumers were direct. The producers of the local markets displayed their wares by shouting and giving samples for promoting their trade; and as such there was no special need for advertising.

British settlement and ruling brought about certain changes in our country. British needed advertising efforts to popularize their goods, particularly the luxury goods. The first printing press was established by the Portuguese in 1556, which was used exclusively for printing Christian literature. It was only in 1780 that the first Indian newspaper started, namely the 'Bengal Gazette' in Calcutta. By 1786, there were four weekly newspapers and a few monthlies published from Calcutta. It was in the 'Bengal Journal' that all the government advertisements of that period were printed. 'The Courier' which was published from Bombay during that period also contained advertisement in various Indian languages, namely Marathi, Gujarati, Konkani, Urdu and Kannada. In 1791, 'The Government Gazette' was started in which all the government advertisements in different provincial languages were printed. Though the first newspaper in an Indian language started in 1833, it took a pretty longer time to put advertisements in Indian languages newspaper. There were no advertising agencies; but, the newspapers had provided the services of space selling.

The eighteenth century saw the advent of 'classified advertising' in India. Initially advertisements were imported from the studios of England; but, later indigenous newspaper studios were developed in India which brought together copywriters, visualizers, illustrators and various other creative artistes.

A lot of British retailers and medicine manufacturers comprised the major clientele for these studios. Retailers advertised their imported products in the form of lists. The success of this advertising format led to the growth of 'mail-order advertising' wherein retailers published thick catalogues of their products carrying information and promotional offers.

Commercial advertising in India commenced in 1905 with the establishment of 'B. Dattaram and Co.' – the first advertising agency in the country. The pre-independence era saw a rather slow growth in the Indian advertising scenario.

Newspaper circulation increased during the First World War with the growing interest among the readers in news of the war. Newspaper advertising got a fillip when the Indian market was flooded with foreign goods in the post war period as much space was booked for advertising. The British and the American agencies posed tough competition for domestic agencies; eventually leading to their failure. The Indian agencies saw potential in advertising business as a rich source of earning and employment.

'Tats Publicity' (1918), started by a Bombay based British army officer, was the first professional modern advertising agency, followed by D. Jekey More's agency (1929) and the 'Thompson Advertising Agency' (early 1930's).[12] Indian advertising got another break during the 'Swadeshi Movement' as it led to the popularisation of Indian goods against the imported ones through widespread advertising.

The Indian advertising scenario has had many changing phases. The pre-independence advertisements were mostly about goods, clothes hotels, restaurants, cars and luxury items as the target audience were mainly the British in India, the royal families and the upper class elite strata of the society. It was only after the abolition of the princely order post-independence that the middle class caught the attention of advertisers. Advertising agencies flourished from 14 in 1914 to 45 agencies in 1944. However, the gross income was just Rs. 5 crore; indicating the slow growth of the business in the country. The other reasons for the slow growth were the lack of industrialization, limited market and lack of competition.[14]

The first full-fledged Indian advertising agency was set up in 1934 – 'The Sista Advertising and Publicity Services'.[15] The increased competition demanded a thorough improvement in the quality of advertising work and services. To improve the art-work and copy illustration, Indian agencies used to send their employees abroad for a special training. 'The All India Radio' started broadcasting various programmes in 1936. In 1939, 'The Indian and Eastern Newspaper Society' was founded to protect and promote the legitimate interests of the newspapers and to deal collectively with the government, agencies and the advertisers.

Advertising during those days got a fillip; with media becoming more organised and also with the formation of media syndicates. With India becoming a note-worthy market for products, advertisements for many multinational products like 'Lux' and 'Horlicks' were Indianised.[12]

'The Indian Languages Newspapers Association' was formed in 1941 to deal with the problems of Indian language newspapers. The political and economic scene underwent a sweeping change by the end of the Second World War. Consequently, the scarcity conditions prevailing in the Indian economy gave much impetus to the growth and development of light and small industries. In 1945, 'The Association of Advertising Agencies of India' (A.A.A.1) was formed to raise the standard of advertising and regulation of advertising practices through a code of conduct. The Audit Bureau of Circulations of India (A.B.C.1) was started in 1948 on the lines of 'The A.B.C' of America. In 1952, 'The Indian society of Advertisers' was formed in 1952, to promote the interests of advertisers so as to raise the standard of Indian advertising. After independence, the Five Year Plans were implemented and several factories and large - scale projects have emerged and this marked the beginning of the 'Golden Age' of advertising in India. Advertisements in the Indian Print media achieved a considerable importance only from the beginning of the twentieth century. Educational development and the popularization of media had also contributed much to the expansion in the field of advertising in India. 'The Advertisers' Club of Bombay' was started in 1954 and such clubs had emerged later in all the metropolitan cities in India. The telecasting of programmes through television had commenced in India on 15th September 1959 at Delhi. Besides these, there are some other forms of publicity used by the advertisers, which include the use of short films, slide shows, messages on the radio and in television. Television advertising has become as popular today in India, as it is in other parts of the world. Film advertising in India has attained popularity among both the advertisers and the consumers because the advertisers can advertise their products even in the remotest corners of the country using cinema theatres as the medium.

The 1960s saw an upsurge of creativity in Indian advertising industry. This was inspired by the transformation of advertising at the international level into a more modern scientific approach. The creative 'Volkswagen' campaigns promoted the concept of 'positioning' or 'unique selling proposition' internationally. 'ITC' in India made records with its 1963 slogan 'Made for each other' for 'Wills' cigarettes.[16] Similarly, in 1964, Lifebuoy's 'Tandurusti ki raksha' (protection of health) campaign was very successful. In 1967, Amul hit the jackpot with its hoarding campaign featuring the polka-dot-dressed moppet that entertained viewers with her topic-based humour. The campaign finds a mention in the Guinness Book of World Records as the longest running outdoor campaigns.

Radio advertising has been introduced by the 'Vividh Bharti' (All-India Radio) at Bombay from 1st November 1967.[17] This pilot project was started with commercials being put over low power 'Vividh Bharati' transmitters at Bombay, Poona and Nagpur. It gained widespread popularity among the traders and industrialists.

The year 1976-77 was a turning point in the history of Indian advertising. It was in this year that 'The Doordarshan' (DD) started accepting advertisements. Commercial advertising on television was introduced in a small way on 1st January 1976 and the revenue from commercial advertising has shot up at an astronomical rate leading to a flood of sponsored programmes and the opening of a second channel in Delhi and Bombay. The first burst of public sector advertising was in the 1980s; but, what catapulted the industry on to a higher plank was the landmark launch of colour television on August 15th 1982. Colour printing in newspapers and magazines also brought about a new hue to their readability. To proclaim the serious role of advertising in competitive scenarios, the Advertising Standards Council of India (ASCI) was born. The 1980's also witnessed the first round of sponsored television programming.

The Indian advertising industry has come a long way from Rs.100 million industry (1955) to Rs.1600 million (1978) to Rs.50,000 million (1999). Satellite television has phenomenally influenced the style and substance of advertising. Globalisation, privatization and liberalization have created both challenges and opportunities for advertising with the increase of fierce competition.

The concept of market research in advertising was pioneered by 'Hindustan Lever' in rural India. 'Hindustan Thompson Associates (HTA) and 'Lintas' followed the trend. The total advertising turnover in 1994-95 was of Rs.775 crores; wherein Doordarshan had a share of Rs. 400 crore, Rs. 200 crores was advertised on the network and the remaining Rs.175 crores on the the satellite channels.[18]

Online advertising is has also gained momentum after globalisation in India. India's online advertising revenues increased from $2.5 million (1999) to $150 million (2003).[14]

With the advancements in colour processing and printing technology, the Indian advertisers were successful in bringing out advertisements of international standards in various print media.

An analysis of the growth of advertising industry in India from the year 1985 to 2003 shows that the industry has shown a steady growth from Rs.580 crores (1985) to 15000 crores (2003).[19]

Lynne Ciochetto, in her book, '*Globalisation and advertising in emerging economies: Brazil, Russia, India and China*' summarizes the impact of globalisation on Indian television advertising.[20] In the early 1990s, there was a massive expansion in advertising in India when the government relaxed the regulations on foreign company advertising on Indian television. The advertising of foreign products on television was not permitted until 1994. At the same time there was a proliferation of television channels including satellite channels. Quoting various sources, Ciochetto mentioned that advertising expenditure increased from $415 in 1992 to $1748 million in 2001 with a slight dip in 1998 with the Asian economic crisis. The advertising industry further expanded since 2000 and advertising expenditure in 2006 was at $4.1 billion.

Ciochetto mentions that the advertising in India was dominated by Indian agencies until the 1990s because of government limitations on foreign ownership. By 1992-93, 11 out of 20 Indian agencies were affiliated with multinational agencies. By 1999, there were about 400 advertising agencies in India and 15 of the top 20 advertising agencies in India had affiliations or joint ventures with foreign agencies.

With the proliferation of television channels after the liberalisation and globalisation policies of the 1990s, a steady growth in television advertising was also noticed. The first foreign companies to move in were the fast moving consumer goods like personal products, cigarettes, soft drinks and pharmaceuticals. Further, the rising disposable income levels were reflected in the increased advertising for consumer durables. In 1993, 75 per cent of television advertisements were for five major groups of products: toiletries and detergents, cold drinks, food products, cosmetics and health products.

Post globalisation, advertising in India has largely been dominated by the foreign companies. The competition further increased with these foreign companies taking over the local brands. Fierce competition was witnessed in the three key product categories: soap, detergents and soft-drinks; with Procter & Gamble, Unilever (HLL) and Colgate Palmolive competition in the soaps and detergent front while Coca-Cola and Pepsi taking the soft-drink industry by storm.

Ciochetto, successfully elucidating on the impact of advertising on the culture of India, states that the expansion of advertising contributes to the processes of social and cultural change that have accompanied the accelerated globalisation of the economy since the 1990s. Post liberalisation, advertising has contributed to cultural change through the introduction of new values like individualism and intensification of other values like materialism and consumerism; thereby diminishing key values of the society. It has been alleged that such trend has led to the undermining of traditional habits and behaviours, creation of new wants and desires and the re-formulation of cultural values and beliefs. In 1980, UNESCO compiled a report, documenting key values promoted through advertising which included consumerism, materialism, individualism, hedonism, sexuality apart from stereotyping body types and gender roles.

Today, advertising is once again on the crossroads. Innovations like guerrilla marketing are underway which includes interactive advertising where the viewers can interact with the advertiser and respond to the messages, staged encounters of products in public places, narrowcast of advertisements on 'Direct To Home' screens, transmission of messages on small screens of hand held devices; and more. While its form may change; advertising is here to stay.[16]

References

1 Bootwala, S., Lawrence, M. D., & Mali, S. R. (2007). *Advertising and Sales Promotion*. Pune: Nirali Prakashan.

2 Jain, A. (2009). *Principles of Marketing*. VK Publications.

3 Trehan, M., & Trehan, R. (2007). *Advertising and Sales Management*. FK Publications.

4 *History of Advertising - An overview*. (n.d.). Retrieved from http://ietd.inflibnet.ac.in/ bitstream/10603/375/7/07_chapter2.pdf

5 Gupta, O. (2005). *Advertising in India: Trends and Impact*. Gyan Publishing House.

6 Kazmi, S. H., & Batra, S. K. (2008). *Advertising & Sales Promotion*. New Delhi: Excel Books.

7 Pitch Madison Advertising Report 2016 - http://www.exchange4media.com / pmar2016/pmar-report.pdf

8 http://www.livemint.com/Consumer/ZMMO64fyHGq0VT0Lbb8qJJ/Ad-spending-in-India-to-grow-at-10-in-2017-GroupM-report.html

9 Mandell, M. I. (1974). *Advertising*. Englewood Cliffs, NJ: Prentice-Hall.

10 Ingham, J. N. (1983). *Biographical dictionary of American business leaders: [1]*. Westport, CT: Greenwood Press.

11 McDonough, J., & Egolf, K. (2015). *The Advertising age encyclopedia of advertising*. New York: Routledge.

12 Douglas, T. (1986). *The complete guide to advertising*. Papermac.

13 Medoff, N. J., & Kaye, B. K. (2010). *Electronic media: Then, now, and later*. Taylor & Francis.

14 *Chapter-1 Introduction*. (n.d.). Retrieved from http://shodhganga.inflibnet.ac.in /bitstream/10603/72959/10/10_chapter%201.pdf

15 Srivastava, A. (n.d.). Advertising History. Retrieved from https://www.scribd.com /doc/21560255/ Evaluation-of-indian-Advertising-History

16 Shah, K. (2014). *Advertising and integrated marketing communicatons*. New Delhi: McGraw Hill Education (India.

17 *Milestones of All India Radio*. (n.d.). Retrieved from http://allindiaradio.gov.in/profile /milestones/pages/default.aspx

18 Agarwal, A. (1995, March 31). Battling for the big bucks. Retrieved from http://indiatoday.intoday.in/story/despite-competition-from-private-channels-doordarshan-survives-eyes-increase-in-revenues/1/288511.html

19 *Advertising & Child*. (n.d.). Retrieved from http://shodhganga.inflibnet.ac.in/ bitstream /10603/92565/10/10_chapter2.pdf

20 Ciochetto, L. (2013). *Globalisation and advertising in emerging economies: Brazil, Russia, India and China*. (Vol.51) Routledge.

2

Advertising Ethics
An Overview

Ethics are moral principles and values that govern the actions of individuals or group.[1] In other words ethics is the branch of social science that deals with moral principles and values.[2] It helps us differentiate the good from the bad. The good is expected to be retained; discarding the bad.

There are various ethical issues in advertising ranging from the question of validity of claims made in the advertisements, the content and their presentation; some important issues being advertising of harmful products, gender bias, portraying of women in bad light, unhealthy brand comparison among others.

S.S. Kaptan, in his book, '*Advertising, New concepts*' very aptly summarises the ethical issues concerning advertising.[2] He states that advertising's main purpose is to make customers aware of new products and services and to persuade them to buy the same. Given the fact that advertising differs from the news media and need not follow the same ethical standard; but, it is always expected that it sticks to truth as people have a tendency to take it on face value and gullibly believe all or most of what is said. The definition of truth in this case should be leaving out of any false statements used in an effort to deceive the potential consumer. Some of the most common ways of deception are mentioned as follows:

1. *Exaggeration*: Tall claims are often made by advertisers to promote their products; mainly, those of detergent powders, cosmetics and toiletries.
2. *Misuse of testimonials*: Testimonial is a statement given by a popular personality or any other ambassador claiming the superiority of the brand. The fact remains that the advertisers end up paying hefty amount of money to extract that statement from them; and it might so happen that the person has never actually used the product.
3. *Free gifts and discounts*: We have all come across advertisements such as 'pay for two and take three', 'buy one get one free', '50% discount' or 'participate in some contests and win handsome prizes'. Most of such

advertising are tricks to fool innocent customers as most of the free gift products are not worth the mentioned price and in case of a discounted sale; the products may be damaged or of old stock or of inferior quality.

4. *Misrepresentation:* One comes across competitive brands with similar names like Haldiram and Haldirams or Aggarwal Sweets and Agarwal Sweets or Godrej and Gordrej etc. There are some other brands that fancies 'made in China' or 'made in Japan' tags to fool the customers and manipulate the prices of the goods.
5. *False statistics*: There are also advertisers who make use of false statistics to vouch for the superiority of their goods. For instance, most of the home-shopping products feature statements like 'Million products already sold out; grab the last few pieces now'; but in reality very few pieces might have actually been sold off.
6. *Total lies*: There are also cases wherein the advertisers present blatant lies to lure customers into buying their products. They use slogans like 'Get instant fairness' or 'lose weight in one week' etc.
7. *Poor taste*: At times some brands present vulgar advertisements that include sexual innuendos, double meanings or nudity. Examples of such ads are that of Rotomac pens – 'sab kuch dikhta hai' (Everything can be seen) or Amul macho – 'ye toh bada toing hai' (suggesting sex appeal) etc.
8. *Unhealthy brand comparisons*: Nowadays, advertisers are engaged in unhealthy brand comparisons. One brand is seen derogating another one for its own promotion. This practice is completely unethical as a brand is supposed to bank on its own strengths and not by pulling another brand down the ladder. Examples of such unhealthy comparisons are that of Complan and Horlicks, Colgate and Pepsodent or Dabur honey and Patanjali honey etc.
9. *Surrogate advertising*: The Cable Television Networks Rules, 1999 prohibits companies from advertising tobacco and liquor; leaving surrogate advertising as their last resort. Such companies usually either go for brand extension and promote the extended products, or promote certain products which might not be available in the market. The excessive pressure of the ban forced companies to focus more on brand building and thus liquor companies started sponsoring and hosting glamorous events, yet many others started distributing t-shirts, caps, key chains, drinking glasses with the brand name displayed on these products. Charles W. Lamb, in his book, '*Marketing*'[3] cites the example of the 'UB Group' that markets 'Kingfisher beer' and 'Royal Challenge whisky' that bought the Indian Cricket Team and named it 'Royal Challengers'. The colour and logo of the team are same

as the whisky brand. Similarly, the 'Bacardi Martini India' sells a line of music CDs with the brand name 'Bacardi Blast'.

10. *Suppression of important information*: Companies generally have the tendency to highlight only the positive aspects of their products and services. The biggest deception is suppression of information that might be of immense relevance to the customers. A very common example is labelling of eatables as 'Fat free'. These food products may be fat free; but, they may have very high cholesterol; which the advertisers suppress. A lay man would not know that unburned cholesterol would ultimately be fat. Thus, it is essential that companies highlight both the pros and cons of their products and let the consumers judge what is best for them.
11. *Subliminal advertising*: Sangeeta Sharma and Raghuvir Singh, in their book, '*Advertising: Planning and implementation*' stated about the impact of subliminal advertising in human consciousness.[4]

The term 'subliminal' means below the threshold of consciousness.[5] The idea is that certain things that are seen, heard or felt never reach our conscious thought process; but, are recorded somewhere in our sub conscious mind; and have an impact on our decisions and behaviour. Advertising professionals use this concept to hide messages within advertisements; which eventually manipulates the behaviour of the target audience without even them realising the same.

Vir Bala Aggarwal and V.S. Gupta, in their book, '*Handbook of Journalism and Mass Communication*' writes that the advertising industry has made rapid strides especially since the early nineties. The policy of economic liberalisation and growth of economy have largely been contributory factors apart from technological advances.[6]

It has been observed that the Indian advertising industry has been frequently criticised for putting out misleading and exaggerated claims in respect of products, goods and services advertised. It has also been perceived as guilty of glorifying certain undesirable or unethical elements and promoting consumerist culture. This has often led to demands for stricter norms, regulations and laws. Currently, the Indian advertising industry promises to meet the situation through a system of self-regulation.

The one general difficulty about self-regulation is its enforcement and implementation. In this context K.S. Venkateswaran in his book, '*Mass Media Laws And Regulations in India*' says, "Exaggerated claims, appalling bad taste, economy of truth in providing information about products and services; and a general lack of concern for consumer's interest have given the industry a bad side to its reputation which it could do without."[7]

Advertising related Laws in India

The Government of India has not set up a regulatory body in India to regulate advertisements. But as in due course depending on the nature of the grievances, the power to regulate advertisements may be exercised by a vast variety of authorities, including the courts, Central and state governments, tribunals or the police authorities. In addition to that, numerous legislations also deal with advertisement provisions in part, unfortunately, though not in total. The major rules, regulations and legislations include:

- Constitution of India;
- Indian Penal Code, 1860;
- The Contract Act, 1872;
- The Drugs and Cosmetics Act, 1940;
- The Emblems and Names (Prevention of Improper Use) Act, 1950;
- The Drugs and Magic Remedies (Objectionable Advertisements) Act, 1955;
- The Young Persons (Harmful Publications) Act, 1956;
- The Civil Defense Act, 1968
- The Cigarettes (Regulation of Production, Supply and Distribution) Act, 1975;
- Consumer Protection Act, 1986;
- Indecent Representation of Women (Prohibition) Act, 1986;
- Securities and Exchange Board of India (SEBI) (Stock-brokers and Sub-brokers) Rules, 1992;
- The Infant Milk Substitutes, Feeding Bottles and Infant Foods (Regulation of Production, Supply and Distribution) Act, 1992;
- The Prenatal Diagnostic Techniques (Regulation and Prevention of Misuse) Act, 1994;
- The Transplantation of Human Organs Act, 1994;
- Code of Conduct for Stock-brokers, Securities and Exchange Board of India (SEBI) (Prohibition of Fraudulent and Unfair Trade Practices relating to Securities Market) Regulations, 1995;
- Securities and Exchange Board of India (SEBI) (Mutual Funds Regulation), 1996;
- The Representation of the People (Amendment) Act, 1996;
- The Lotteries (Regulation) Act, 1998;
- Information Technology Act, 2000;
- SEBI Guidelines for Advertisements by Mutual Funds, Securities and Exchange Board of India (SEBI) (Disclosure and Investor Protection Guidelines), 2000;

- The Competition Act, 2002;
- The Cigarettes and other Tobacco Products (Prohibition of Advertisement and Regulation of Trade and Commerce, Production, Supply and Distribution) Act, 2003 and
- Advertising Standards Council of India (ASCI) among others.[8]

The important ones (Laws) are discussed as follows:

1. *Constitution of India*

The Constitution of India does not directly deal with advertising ethics but it has certain provisions that deal with children, non-discrimination based on skin colour, promotion of communal harmony and fostering of peaceful foreign relations among many others that deal with our area of study.

2. *The Advertising Standards Council of India*

We have, in India, the ASCI – The Advertising Standards Council of India – a self regulatory voluntary organization of the Advertising Industry that works on the mission to maintain and enhance the public's confidence in advertising. ASCI, established in 1985, was formed with the support of all four sectors connected with advertising, viz. advertisers, advertising agencies, media (including broadcasters and the press) and others like PR agencies, market research companies etc. 'The Consumer Complaints Council' is ASCI's heart and soul. It is the dedicated work put in by this group of highly respected people that has given tremendous impetus to the work of ASCI and the movement of self- regulation in the advertising industry.[9] (*Refer Annexure - I*)

3. *Indian Penal Code, 1860*

The code provides punishment for offences against the State as well as those affecting the society, human body, property, reputation, public tranquillity, public justice, religion among others. With regards to our area of study, Sections 292, 293 and 294 of the IPC deals with laws relating to obscene representations; and Sections 153A, 295 and 295A deals with non-discrimination based on religion. (*Refer Annexure - II*)

4. *Indecent Representation of Women (Prohibition) Act, 1986*

This legislation relates to representation of women in Indian media. With regards to our area of study, Section 3 of the Act deals with prohibition of advertisements containing indecent representation of women.

5. *Cable Television Networks (Regulation) Act, 1995*

With the boom of cable television in 1990s, the government of India felt the necessity to enact a piece of legislation that could pose a barrier to undesirable programmes and advertisements which were becoming available to viewers without any kind of censorship. With regards to our area of study, under this Act the ministry may issue directions to television channels or cable TV operators to stop airing an ad and not to the advertisers.

6. *Cable television networks rules, 1994*

It is necessary that all service providers shall adhere to the Programme code and the Advertising code prescribed under the rules.

7. *Press Council of India's Norms for Journalistic ethics*

These codes are divided into four parts which deal with principles and ethics, guidelines on specific issues, laws relating to press and the powers, practices and procedures of the Press Council. With regards to our areas of study, the norms deal with right to privacy of an individual, fostering of communal harmony, promoting good foreign relations and also non-discrimination of the LGBT (lesbian, gay, bi-sexual and trans-gender) community.

References

1 Trehan, M., & Trehan, R. (2007). *Advertising and Sales Management.* FK Publications.

2 Kaptan, S. S. (2002). *Advertising, New Concepts.* New Delhi: Sarup & Sons.

3 Crompton, J. L., & Lamb, C. W. (1986). *Marketing Government and Social Services.* New York: Wiley.

4 Sharma, S., & Singh, R. (2006). *Advertising: Planning and Implementation.* PHI Learning Pvt. Ltd.

5 Cacioppo, J. T., & Freberg, L. (2015). *Discovering Psychology: The Science of Mind.* Nelson Education.

6 Aggarwal, V. B., & Gupta, V. S. (2001). *Handbook of Journalism and Mass Communication.* New Delhi: Concept Publishing Company.

7 Venkateswaran, K. S., & Asian Mass Communication Research and Information Centre. (1993). *Mass media laws and regulations in India.*

8 Pathak, J. P. (2014). *Introduction to Media Laws and Ethics.* Delhi: Shipra Publications.

9 The Advertising Standards Council of India. (n.d.). Retrieved from http://www.ascionline.org/images/pdf/asci_code_new.pdf

3

Advertising Vis-A-Vis Child Rights

Advertisements through Unclad Babies

Child is an asset and future resource of manpower of a nation. Its development with dignity is a matter of great concern throughout the world. The Indian Constitution has also taken care of child by providing the following provisions in Article 39 of the Directive Policies[1].

The state shall, in particular, direct its policy towards securing:

1. The health and strength of workers, and that children are not abused at the tender age and that citizens are not forced by economic necessity to enter vocations unsuited to their age or strength,
2. That children are given opportunities and facilities to develop in a healthy manner and in a condition of freedom and dignity and that childhood and youth are protected against exploitation, and against moral and material abandonment.

The United Nations 'Convention on the Rights of the Child'[2], which has been adopted by the General Assembly of the United Nations on 20th November, 1989 and also acceded by the Government of India in the Convention dated 11th December, 1992, provides for provisions for the welfare and procedure for punishment.

The Government of India, in pursuance of the constitutional provisions, evolved a 'National policy for the welfare of children'. This policy starts with a goal-oriented introduction: 'The nation's children are a supremely important asset. Their nature and solicitude are our responsibility. Children's programme should find a prominent part in our national plans for the development of human resources, so that our children grow up to become robust citizens, physically fit, mentally alert and morally healthy, endowed with skills and motivations, needed by society. Equal opportunities for development to all children during the period of growth should be our aim, for this would serve our larger purpose of reducing inequality and ensuring social justice.'[3]

But even though we have so many international and national laws to protect the rights of the child, certain seemingly minor aspects are being overlooked which can be a major violation in the rights of a child.

Exploitation of Children

Any form of exploitation of children, that has a tendency to exploit them either physically, mentally or otherwise, is objectionable. The various provisions of the constitution, particularly Articles 21, 39, 41, 45 and 46 reflect the goals set by our constitution makers that all attempts in the direction of exploitation of children must be put to an end.

Many debates have been going on for a long time whether children acting in advertisements or other media related platform can also be considered as child labourers. With the rise of the question many Acts and laws in the name of protecting the child against exploitation also came up. But, nothing contained therein speaks of protecting the dignity of a child whose private parts are being exposed in the television through advertisements. Is it not exploitation of the body of the child? Just because the child is too small to speak for itself and the audience enjoy seeing the cuteness of their bodies, they should not be shown unclad on television.[4]

Even the mannequins are being covered properly before they are being dressed or while changing their outfits, then is it not the duty of media and advertisement professionals to protect the dignity of the child and not expose body parts of the child that can be a reason of embarrassment for the child at a later stage in life.

Children and their Welfare

To quote a small incident, there is one video in YouTube that shows Princess Diana and Prince Charles with baby William. They were playing with the baby, but, it suddenly began to wriggle in uneasiness. The princess immediately got up and took the baby inside to change its clothes as it had pissed out. The Prince too, immediately stood up and told the cameraman that he could smell something; so they would only be back after the clothes of the baby were changed.

This gesture of the mother of upholding the right to privacy of the baby is a matter of appreciation. She could have changed the baby's diaper there, too, where they were sitting; thinking that it was only a baby and that there is no problem in changing the diaper; but, instead, she protected his dignity and self-esteem by not exposing him in front of the camera; and thereby to the public.

Children need special protection because of their tender age, mental immaturity and incapacity to look after themselves. There is a growing realisation in every part of the globe that children must be brought up with love, affection, dignity and under tender care and attention, so that they may be able to attain full emotional, intellectual and spiritual stability and maturity and acquire self confidence and self respect.

There has been equally great concern for the welfare of the children at the international level culminating in the Declaration of Rights of the Child adopted by the General Assembly of the United Nations.[5] The Declaration in its preamble points out that the child by reason of his physical and mental immaturity needs special safeguards and care including appropriate legal protection, before as well as after birth and that mankind owes to the child the best it has to give and proceeds to formulate several principles. It provided that the child shall enjoy special protection and shall be given opportunities and facilities, by law and by other means, to enable him to develop physically, mentally, morally, spiritually and socially in a healthy and normal manner and in conditions of freedom and dignity. In the enactment of law for this purpose, the best interest of the child shall be the paramount consideration.[5]

The exposure of the child in advertisements on television is detrimental to the dignity of the child or the baby. The gender of the child might not be shown on screen but it should be kept in mind that during the shooting of the advertisements the child or the baby is exposed to the cast and crew; and that the baby is handled by complete strangers; and there is no scope to assure that baby is not manhandled, exploited or harassed during the process.

A baby is like a doll that cannot differentiate between right and wrong. Even if it is exploited or harassed on the sets during the unclad state, it will not be able to defend itself or protect itself from it.

Ms. Kalyani *Das*, member of Assam State Commission for Protection of Child Rights said, "We can go further in-depth into the case and think of untoward happenings like what if the cuteness of the baby lures people to click its pictures or make videos in that unclad state which might later be used for child pornography? I was in USA to see my baby grand-child. I clicked some of her photographs while she was having bath in the tub. Her nanny immediately asked me to delete the photos and told me that the law in the nation was very strict and if anybody saw photos of a nude baby on my phone or camera, I might be arrested of being involved in child pornography. I was shocked, but happy at the same time that the law there was so stringent to protect the dignity of the child."

Content Analysis of Advertisements

1. A Huggies diaper advertisement that features Kajol with a baby shows that the baby follows the shadow of its mother (Kajol) who directs the kid to see its own shadow on the floor; and she rushes to get her video camera to record the baby playing with its own shadow. But as soon as she starts recording, she finds that the baby is sitting in a puddle of toilet. The voice over says, "Bacche har pal naye koshisho me joote rehte hai lekin gile pan ke vajah se un koshishon me rukawat aasakti hai. Isiliye le aayiye Huggies…" (Children are always attempting to perform new things but dampness can be a hurdle in their efforts... thus, buy Huggies). She shuts the video off and changes the kid to Huggies Diaper. The advertisement ends with a note, "Gilapan nahi toh koshishen kayi" (No dampness means more efforts).
2. Another advertisement of the product, *Huggies Wonder Pants*, featuring Kajol with a baby starts with the mother (Kajol) cladding the bare baby with the product and then starts playing with the baby. The baby crawls away from the mother in a fast pace that the mother gets apprehensive that it will hit the wooden frame of the bed but luckily the baby strikes its head against the pillow and is safe much to the relief of the mother. The voice over says, "Bacchon ke liye komalta bhari suraksha se badhkar aur kya ho sakta hai?" (What more can be important to babies but soft protection?).
3. Yet another product, *Huggies Care*, in its advertisement shows a mother and the baby playing hide and seek. The mother finds the baby but is shocked to see him sitting on its own toilet and splashing it with its hands.
4. *Huggies Dry Comfort*, in its advertisement shows a boy running around bare bottom and a song, 'Coochikoo' plays in the background. Everyone in the family fiddles with the buttocks of the child which tries to signify that it is soft and dry because it uses the product.
5. *Huggies Dry Pants* advertises its product and shows the bare bottom of the child with rashes to make the parents aware that it is important to keep the private parts of the baby clean and dry so suggests them to use their product.
6. In another advertisement of *Huggies Total Protection* product, the mother kisses the child on its bare bottom.
7. *Mamy Poko Pants* in its advertisements of pant styled diapers shows how the diaper of a baby opens up as it is ill fitting. An animated character suggests that diapers should be pant styled so that it fits well

and keeps the baby comfortable. It also uses an unclad baby in the advertisement.

8. *Pampers Active Baby* advertisements also uses unclad babies. In one such advertisement of their pant styled diapers, the baby is seen in an unclad state.
9. In one *Pampers Good Morning* advertisement, the baby is shown getting up with a smile on its face and the mother is proud that her baby always gets up with a smile because it wears diapers from Pampers. This advertisement does not show babies in an unclad state.
10. One *Huggies* advertisement features a child playing with a ball of wool that slipped away from the mother's hand who was knitting a sweater. The advertisement does not show the baby in an unclad state and just portrays how happy the child is playing with its parents while putting on the advertised product that is keeping it dry.

As we see, except in the last two cases, all other advertisements have shown the babies in an unclad state.

Now, the question is why babies should be shown in an exposed state when the message can be sent even with fully clothed babies? Their right to privacy is violated when they are shown in negative light; like sitting on and splashing their own toilet. Babies cannot speak for themselves and the elders should respect their privacy and protect their self respect.

Interviews

During the course of research, author has spoken/contacted to:

1. Ms. Kalyani Das, member of the Assam State Commission for Protection of Child Rights. She said,
   "The topic of the research is very new and it is important that we take such subtle aspects into consideration. I have been working for the protection of the rights of the children for so long but this angle of thought never struck my mind. It is indeed true that the rights of those babies are being violated for personal and business gains. And it is necessary that some action is taken against it."
2. Ms. Kalyani Das referred the name of Ms. Urmimala Sengupta who is the Consultant for Assam State Commission for Protection of Child Rights. She said,
   "I believe this is the first time somebody has thought of this aspect of the violation of child rights. It has never been thought of before and I am sure this step will bring to light that such subtle thing that goes unnoticed can also have important impression on the life of a

child. The aspect of advertising is still in its budding stage in India and India itself is developing. So, we have to wait for many more years for people to understand the importance of such things. Exposing a baby on camera for the whole nation to see and that too in a negative light, like making it sit on a puddle of toilet which is an artificially created scene is definitely a violation of their rights to privacy and self esteem. Their dignity is being harmed in this way and some action should be urgently taken to put a stop to it. But then again, unless its importance is being highlighted in the media, it is hard to say when the time will come when people will themselves realize what harm they are causing to the dignity of the little ones who cannot speak for themselves."

3. Ms. Kalyani Das referred the name of Mr. Ved Prakash Gautam, Child Protection Officer , UNICEF, Guwahati.
   When asked to give his inputs on the topic concerned, all he said was, "For such queries write to Ms. Suchorita Bardhan, Communication officer, UNICEF, Assam, with CC to jmaster@unicef.org."
4. Ms. Dipa Dixit, member of National Commission for Protection of Child Rights said,
   "Thank you for your kind mail. As I mentioned that the broadcasters have set up a self regulatory body - The Broadcasting Content Complaints Council (BCCC) in consultation with the Ministry of Information & Broadcasting. the Council has a chairperson Justice (Retd.) A.P. Shah and members which consists of experts, representatives from the Broadcasters, representatives from various Govt. Commissions, etc. The Council regulates content of TV programs through its own guidelines. I am sending you Mr. Ashish Sinha's email id (Secretary-BCCC) and am copying him in on this mail. You may consider calling him for the clarifications that you need for your paper. You may give him my reference."
5. Mr. Ashish Sinha (Secretary-BCCC) said,
   "Thanks for writing to us! However, let me clarify that the Broadcasting Content Complaints Council (BCCC) does not look into advertisement-related complaints. Our jurisdiction extends only to complaints related to content of programmes aired on non-news channels. The competent body for examining ad-related complaints is Advertising Standards Council of India (ASCI) (www.ascionline.org). The person to be contacted is Mr. Alan Collaco, Secretary General, ASCI."
   He is right that the Broadcasting Content Complaints Council (BCCC) does not look into advertisement-related complaints, but then, when

one authority recommends another authority; we must doubt if they are aware of their jurisdiction of work.

7. Mr. Alan Collaco, Secretary General, ASCI never responded to my email, nor did any response come from the email id that they provided for lodging complaints against advertisements.
8. To take the opinion of a psychiatrist, Prof. Dr. Devakumar, M.D., Registered Psychologist and Psychiatrist and Honorary Advisor to American Biographical Institute, USA was contacted. He said,

   "Let me throw some experiences of mine. When I meet ordinary children, I find that there is a change of behaviour in them when they apply make-up and then they change into something else. I have seen pretty girl children turning into fairies after putting on make-up. They have a change of behaviour on the spot. We would not have thought of such a happening might take place. Then there are parents who push the children into modelling of such acts like the ones you said i.e. sitting on a puddle of toilet or letting everyone pamper with their private parts etc. where the children will suffer from inferiority complex later in life. Yes, of course, the parents might do it knowingly or unknowingly that by letting their babies do such acts, they are infringing upon their right to privacy, self-esteem and dignity. But the parents might instead think that it is a thing to be proud of that their babies are into modelling and are being shown endorsing products on national television or media. Through this paper, at least people will realize that how, without anybody realising, the rights of such babies are being violated."

   He also added,

   "Becoming a model at such a tender age might create the urge in them to choose this line as their career and it might also happen that their parents induce them to take up this line as their career choice. We see so many kids coming, working in entertainment business; but, it is very important for their parents and guardians to see that they do not deviate from their studies. Some of such kids, may again, be victim of superiority complexity among other kids of their age or might even suffer from depression, frustration and inferiority complexity; if they see their competitor kids achieving much success than them. So, until they are matured enough to handle their profession in a balanced way, they should not be induced to work in a media that does not guarantee a secured career. Depression might also seep in when later in life they realize that in sought of name and fame they remained educationally unsound. So, there are many angles that need to be noticed and the rights of the children should be protected against them."

9. Delhi office of the NGO, CRY (Child Rights and You) also did not respond.
10. Media Centre of Unilever was contacted to take their justification and opinion for showing unclad babies in the advertisements of their products; but they, too, did not bother to respond. The reason is understood.
11. Johnson and Johnson, India did not respond as well.
12. A similar request was sent to Procter and Gamble regarding the advertisements of the product, Pampers. They were the only company to assure that they will take the complaint into notice. Mo Chu, Consumer Relations Representative of Procter & Gamble replied to email saying, "Thank you for contacting Procter & Gamble regarding Pampers. We always welcome feedback from our consumers as a means of assessing attitudes toward our products and service. We are glad to have the opportunity to respond to your concerns."
13. The former Advocate General of Mizoram and also of Assam and a Senior Advocate in the Gauhati High Court, Mr. Pranab Pathak said,

    "The topic chosen for research is a very unique one and will be a new milestone in safeguarding the rights of the babies who are being exposed to the effect that their rights to privacy, dignity and self esteem are being violated."

    The most important thing that he said was,

    "Babies are Doli Incapax. Black's Law Dictionary defines the term '*Doli Incapax*' as: not being of the age of discretion; not possessed of sufficient discretion and intelligence to distinguish between right and wrong."

    He added,

    "Babies, being Doli Incapax, cannot discriminate between right and wrong and here comes in the role of the parents and the authorities concerned. But parents either are not aware of the implications or it may be that they run after glamour and fame of their wards. And the advertisers would often shirk off saying that they do not see any problem if the parents are ready and willing to portray their babies in that way."
14. Karan Ashar, an actor and model, from Mumbai, who endorses many products said,

    "Well, I think it all depends on the parents. They are responsible for whatever is happening good or bad. That's my view."

15. A few mothers and primary school teachers echoed the view that it is a violation of the rights of the child to be shown unclad through advertisements.
16. Mrs. Tandrali Pathak, an author on theosophy and philosophy said,
    "It is sad that even after 60 years of independence people of India are not aware of their own rights; let alone the rights of others. Men and women, whether from rural or urban areas, are not properly aware of their rights and privileges as citizens of India; furthermore, as just human beings. There are various organs of the United Nations who are working on the field of creating awareness on human rights through international conventions and seminars, but such efforts should be brought down or narrowed down to grass root levels so that the benefits percolate to even the lowest strata of people."
    "I am sure through this study, there will be awareness that, sometimes, looking at bigger things, we overlook certain small, but very important aspects regarding the protection of rights, mainly of the children who cannot speak for themselves."

Analysis from the Interviews

There are many things that came to fore through the interviews done throughout the period of research on this topic. Some of them are:

1. People holding important positions in various child protection centres, whether of the centre or state governments are not fully aware of their roles. They could not respond to the simple question as to what is their opinion on the issue. What most of them did was refer to somebody else for better inputs; who further referred to somebody else making a long chain with no fruitful result.
2. It should be seen that the people holding important positions in various child protection centres regularly check their emails and other means through which general people communicate with them; and that they are provided with the internet. It is meaningless, as well as, unethical when the provided for provisions of emails and phone numbers get obsolete or are never checked.
3. Most companies avoid answering questions that goes against their interest. In this case Procter and Gamble was an exception as they had the courtesy to respond to the query and assuring humbly that they would look into the matter.
4. All the International, National and state bodies working for the protection of the rights of the child should see that their volunteers

and members have thorough knowledge on the subject and are in a position to express their opinion wherever necessary.

5. Some mothers said that the thought that such advertisements can violate the rights of the babies involved never struck their mind. But now that they have realised it, their outlook towards such advertisements have changed.
6. Awareness regarding the rights of children should be done at grass-root level.

Relevant Guidelines on the Protection of the Rights of the Child

The web portal, http://www.unicef.org[6] provides for a factsheet that summarises the important points in the Convention on the Rights of the Child. A few main points are underlined below:

a. Article 3 (Best interests of the child): The best interests of children must be the primary concern in making decisions that may affect them. All adults should do what is best for children. When adults make decisions, they should think about how their decisions will affect children.
b. Article 4 (Protection of rights): Governments have a responsibility to take all available measures to make sure that the children's rights are respected, protected and fulfilled. When countries ratify the Convention, they agree to review their laws relating to children. They must help families protect children's rights and create an environment where they can grow and reach their potential. In some instances, this may involve changing existing laws or creating new ones. Such legislative changes are not imposed, but come about through the same process by which any law is created or reformed within a country.
c. Article 5 (Parental guidance): Governments should respect the rights and responsibilities of families to direct and guide their children so that, as they grow, they learn to use their rights properly. Helping children to understand their rights does not mean pushing them to make choices with consequences that they are too young to handle.
d. Article 16 (Right to privacy): Children have a right to privacy. The law should protect them from attacks against their way of life, their good name, their families and their homes.
e. Article 36 (Other forms of exploitation): Children should be protected from any activity that takes advantage of them or could harm their welfare and development.

f. Article 42 (Knowledge of rights): Governments should make the Convention known to adults and children. Adults should help children learn about their rights, too.

Laws and Codes relating to Advertisements in India:

1. ***Code of Advertising Practice ('ASCI Code')*:** Chapter III Clause 2 states—Advertisements addressed to minors shall not contain anything, whether in illustration or otherwise, which might result in their physical, mental or moral harm or which exploits their vulnerability. (*Refer Annexure - II for examples*)
2. ***Cable Television Networks Rules, 1994*[7]:** Point 7 of the Advertising Code states— No advertisement which endangers the safety of children or creates in them any interest in unhealthy practices or shows them begging or in an undignified or indecent manner shall not be carried in the cable service.
3. ***Press Council of India's Norms for Journalistic ethics*:** Sub-point 10 of Point 36[8] that relates to advertisements state—The editors should insist on their right to have the final say in the acceptance or rejection of advertisements, especially those which border on or cross the line between decency and obscenity.
4. ***CHILDLINE India Foundation*:** CHILDLINE India Foundation (CIF)[9] is the nodal agency of the Union Ministry of Women and Child Development acting as the parent organisation for setting up, managing and monitoring the CHILDLINE 1098 service all over the country. CIF is the sole agency/body responsible for establishing the CHILDLINE service in the cities/districts of the country, monitoring of service delivery and finance, training, research and documentation, creating awareness, advocacy as well as resource generation for the service.[10] They have come out with a law manual, writing elaborately on many important areas where the rights of the children are violated and the laws that are there for protection against the same. But there was no mention of the topic of our study that rights of these babies are also violated when they are shown in an unclad state through advertisements.[11]

   (*The manual can be read at: http://www.childlineindia.org.in/pdf/Law-Manual.pdf*[12])
5. ***Commissions for the Protection of Child Rights Act, 2005*:** This is an Act to provide for the constitution of a National Commission and State Commissions for Protection of Child Rights and Children's

Courts for providing speedy trial of offences against children or of violation of child Rights and for matters connected therewith or incidental thereto.

6. ***The Juvenile Justice (Care and Protection of Children) Act, 2000*:** This Act is the primary legal framework for juvenile justice in India. The Act provides for a special approach towards the prevention and treatment of juvenile delinquency and provides a framework for the protection, treatment and rehabilitation of children in the purview of the juvenile justice system. This law, brought in compliance of Child Rights Convention 1989, repealed the earlier Juvenile Justice Act of 1986 after India signed and ratified Child Rights Convention 1989 in year 1992. This Act has been further amended in year 2006 and 2010. Government of India is once again contemplating bringing further amendments and a review committee has been constituted by Ministry of Women and Child Development which is reviewing the existing legislation. Recent 16 December 2012 Gang rape incident in Delhi has raised a popular demand for amending this law to allow harsher punishments to children involved in serious offences.
7. ***The Child Labour Act, 1986*:** The Act prohibits the employment of children below the age of 14 years in hazardous occupations identified in a list by the law. The list was expanded in 2006, and again in 2008.[13]

Other laws related to the protection of the rights of the child are—

The Factories Act, 1948; The Probation of Offenders Act, 1959; The Child Marriage Restraint Act, 1986; The Right of Children to Free and Compulsory Education Act, 2009; Children Act, 1960[14]*; Children (Pledging of Labour) Act, 1933; Prohibition of Child Marriage Act, 2006; Reformatory Schools Act, 1897 and Young Persons (Harmful Publications) Act, 1956* among others.[15]

Review

After taking an in-depth look at all the laws and codes relating to both advertisements and also to the protection of the rights of the child, we have come to the conclusion that are mentioned as follows:

1. No code of conduct manual relating to advertisements express explicitly that the rights of the child need to be preserved.
2. There is no mention of the rights to privacy, self esteem and dignity of the child.
3. There is no mention that the child portrayed through advertisements should not be shown in a derogatory manner.

Suggestions

We would like to mention certain suggestions that we think can provide some guidelines on the protection of the rights of the children who are portrayed unclad through advertisements. These suggestions are:

1. Organisation like UNICEF should take the matter up and bring it to light so that public and authorities concerned are aware of this aspect through which the rights of the children are being violated.
2. The NGOs should put pressure on the advertising companies to take the matter into notice.
3. The NGOs along with public should put pressure on the government to take the matter into notice and initiate the process of proper legislations on the matter.
4. All the Codes and norms relating to advertising standards should be amended and those provisions that would protect the rights of privacy, self esteem and dignity should be inserted.
5. The media should focus on this aspect so that the public at large is made aware of this violation of child rights.

Conclusion

Children being 'Doli Incapax' do not have the power of discretion. They do not know the difference between right and wrong. Their power to logically think and rationalize is also in a dormant stage. So, it is the duty of the parents, guardians and authorities concerned to see that they are brought up with love, care and dignity.

Children being the pillars of the nation, it is the responsibility of the government to legislate necessary laws that would protect their interest and secure their rights. The companies selling child-related products should take it as their moral responsibility and not show a child in negative light that would harm its interest. All necessary laws should be enacted and other related codes and laws be amended so that they work together for the protection of rights of the child.

The researcher finds that the Indian constitution has a say in the matters of child rights that only deals with their education rights; but, it is absolutely silent on matters of its right to privacy.

It has been found that our Indian Penal Code and the Code of Criminal procedure have sections that deal with punishments for parents who abandon their children wholly (317 of IPC), punishment for kidnapping or abducting children (363 and 369 of IPC), inducing them to beg (363A of IPC), sexual offenders of children (366A of IPC) and procedure to deal with juvenile delinquents (27 of Cr. PC); but there is no mention of punishments or procedure to deal with the right to privacy of a child.

Moreover, the researcher has mentioned about the Child Labour Act of 1986 that prohibits the employment of children under the age of fourteen. But, the Act only prohibits them from working in hazardous occupations identified in a list by the law. Unfortunately, the list does not contain anything related to the protection of the privacy of a child working for television advertisements.

Section 6 of the Press Council of India's Norms of journalistic conduct talks about right to privacy of an individual. It reads that the press shall not intrude upon the privacy of an individual unless outweighed by genuine public interest.

As an explanation, it mentions that the names and photographs of the victims of rape, kidnap or sexual assault should not be published; nor should the names and photographs of minor children or infants who are offsprings of sexual abuse or forcible marriage or illicit sexual union be identified. But, the problem is that the Code prohibits only the 'press' from infringing the right to privacy of women or children. It does not include 'television advertising medium'. The time has come that now, we should broaden the jurisdiction of the Code and include each and every possible outlet of media (including television advertisements); and how they should protect the right to privacy of individuals in their content and output. The lacunas in the Indian legal system regarding the protection of privacy of children working in television advertisements; and all such loop holes should be soon plugged by the relevant authorities so that our children can be safe in whatever environment they are in.

If we all become responsible and work together for the protection of the rights of the child, then our children would feel more secured and protected in our society.

References

1 Basu, D. D. (1971). *Introduction to the Constitution of India*. Calcutta: S.C. Sarkar.

2 McGoldrick, D. (1991). The United Nations convention on the rights of the child. *International Journal of Law, Policy and the Family*, 5(2), 132-169.

3 Kitchlu, T. N. (1996). *Exploited child: A national problem*. New Delhi: M D Publications.

4 P. Pathak, J. (2014). Advertisements through unclad babies vis-à-vis their Child Rights. *IOSR Journal of Humanities and Social Science, 19*(11), 08-17. doi:10.9790/0837-191160817

5 United States. (2002). *The Optional Protocol to the Convention on the Rights of the Child on the Sale of Children, Child Prostitution and Child Pornography and the Optional Protocol to the Convention on the Rights of the Child on the Involvement of Children in Armed Conflict: Report (to accompany Treaty doc. 106-37)*. Washington, D.C.: U.S. G.P.O.

6 *Introducing child protection*. (n.d.). Retrieved from http://www.unicef.org/violencestudy /pdf/CP%20Manual%20-%20Stage%201.pdf

7 *The Cable Television Networks Rules, 1994*. (n.d.). Retrieved from http://www.wipo.int/edocs/lexdocs/laws/en/in/in079en.pdf

8 *Press Council of India Norms of Journalistic Conduct*. (n.d.). Retrieved from http://presscouncil.nic.in/OldWebsite/NORMS-2010.pdf

9 CHILDLINE India Foundation: Child Protection and rights in India, 1098 Child Support. (n.d.). Retrieved from http://www.childlineindia.org.in

10 CHILDLINE India Foundation Website. (n.d.). Retrieved from http://www.childlineindia.org.in/1098/1098.htm

11 CHILDLINE India Foundation - Case Studies. (n.d.). Retrieved from http://www.childlineindia.org.in/1098/b1ecasestudies.htm

12 *Child Rights and Law: a guidebook for legal interventions*. (n.d.). Retrieved from http://www.childlineindia.org.in/pdf/Law-Manual.pdf

13 Bajpai, A. (2003). *Child rights in India: Law, policy, and practice*. New Delhi: Oxford University Press.

14 Van, B. G. (1995). *The international law on the rights of the child*. Dordrecht: M. Nijhoff.

15 Macklin, M. C., & Carlson, L. (1999). *Advertising to Children: Concepts and Controversies*. Sage Publications.

4

Advertising Vis-A-Vis Right to Privacy of Women

Portrayal of Child Delivery

We have all along witnessed in the early Indian movies that when the mother goes into labour pain, the mid-wife would ask for a bucket of hot water and cover the lady with curtains and then there is a cut-away shot; finally letting us hear the cry of the baby so that it is understood by the audience that the baby is born. Later the mid-wife would come out with the baby and announce whether it is a boy or a girl to the father and other relatives in waiting.

The trend of showing the process of normal child delivery started in India, first, in Bollywood movies like 'Salaam Namaste' where actor Preity Zinta delivers a baby. Later, we also saw the same kind of child delivery scene in the movie '3 Idiots' where actor Mona Singh delivers a baby through normal procedure.

But, recently two big companies, the 'MTS Internet Service Provider' and 'Cadbury 5 Star' have started their advertising campaign through the portrayal of women in labour and finally delivering of their babies. These campaigns are being aired on national television and it is felt that such indecent portrayals of women are a strict violation of their right to privacy of women as an entire class.

Advertising and Women

Since market economy runs with the motive of extreme profit; numerous attempts are taken up to promote its business interest.[1] Globalization has facilitated this process. Only marketization can help it sustain in competition. Private enterprises always try to make innovative strategies to sell their products. One such attempt is advertisement. Media barons and conglomerates have flourished manifold. Numerous entertainment channels have sprung up leading to the rise in entertainment programmes and advertisements as well. Advertisement is the tool through which private companies project and promote their commodities. In other words, advertisement helps promote goods for commercial gains.

Products and services are projected to provoke the interest of the public through advertisements. It pushes consumerism into them which in turn serve the interests of multinational corporations. Products like gadgets, electronic and house hold items, chocolates, travel, financial and insurance etc. are advertised to increase the interest of the public in these things; thereby creating prospective customers.

In the advertisements, women are predominantly employed to promote products and services. They are utilized in every item irrespective of whether its presence is required or not. But the recent trend has surpassed all limits. The advertisers have all along been using woman to vouch for their products through their beauty, elegance and sensuality. But now, these advertisers have gone to the extent of exploiting the decency of woman in national television by showing on screen, without any sense of secrecy or veil, the delivering of babies! The producers of goods, in order to sustain themselves and their products in this competitive age, have resorted to derogatory advertisements where they have gone to such a low level where ethics or decency no longer matters.

Right to Privacy

The Indian Constitution does not explicitly guarantee the Right to privacy[2] as a fundamental right. The right to privacy is a rapidly developing concept. It was Thomas Cooley, an American scholar, who, about a century ago, described the Right to privacy as a right to be left alone. The right to privacy has been recognized by the International Convention of Human Rights, 1948. Article 12 of the Universal Declaration of Human Rights states, 'No one shall be subjected to arbitrary interference with his privacy, family, home or correspondence nor to attack upon his honour and reputation. Everyone has the right to the protection of the law against such interference or attacks.'

The power to make these laws is derived from the constitution. 'Privacy' is not a subject in any of the three lists in Schedule VII of the Constitution of India; that is, the State list, the Union list or the Concurrent list. Thus, only the Indian Parliament is competent to legislate on privacy since it can be interpreted as any other matter not enumerated in List II and List III. Till date, there is no specific enactment on the Right to privacy.

Judicial activism has brought the Right to privacy within the realm of Fundamental Rights. Article 141 of the Constitution states that 'the law declared by the Supreme Court shall be binding on all courts within the territory of India.' Therefore, the decisions of the Supreme Court of India becomes the Law of the Land.

The Supreme Court of India has come to the rescue of the common citizens, time and again by construing the Right to privacy as a part of the Fundamental rights for the protection of life and liberty of Indian citizens. Article 21 of the Constitution states, 'No person shall be deprived of his life or personal liberty, except according to procedure established by law.'

Case Studies:

Two case studies are discussed here which became a huge sensation on national television very recently in India.

1. *Mobile TeleSystems (MTS)*

Mobile TeleSystems (MTS), in 2014, had launched a TVC to underline the superiority of its 3G Plus data network, keeping with its focus on the 'net gen.' The film was premiered as a bit-torrent for online audiences to download before digital and social legs kicked in. It was on air from 27 February.[3]

It was on 26th March, 2009 the brand MTS was first launched in the country. As part of its 5th anniversary celebrations, MTS launched the successful MTS' 'Born For the Internet' campaign and offered a free MBlaze Ultra dongle + 10 GB data to all babies born on 26th March 2014.

According to Leonid Musatov, Chief Marketing & Sales Officer – MTS India, "Brand MTS as part of its 5th anniversary celebrations in India wanted to do something unique for data customers.[4] Given the recent success of MTS' 'Born For The Internet' campaign, it was only fitting that we rolled out something as innovative as offering an MBlaze Ultra dongle, bundled with 10 GB data to parents of all babies born on 26th March, 2014."[5]

The TVC portrayed the data superiority of its 3GPlus network in India. The campaign tagline – 'Born for the Internet' – is a reference to both the great data experience of MTS network and to the MTS customer for whom the internet is a way of life.

The TVC stars a 'Born for the internet' baby exploiting the net straight from birth.[6] In a labour room, a woman is being coaxed by the doctor to 'push', while the father and nurses watch anxiously. The baby arrives all of a sudden, with a sound and a jab with its index finger to the doctor's nose. The animated baby rises from under the sheet shocking some of the staff. Grabbing the father's tablet (branded MTS), it searches for 'how to cut the umbilical cord', and then cuts it -- clicking its fingers confidently to get a pair of scissors from the nurse. The baby goes on to take a 'selfie' with the nurse and posts it online. Falling off the bed much to the worry of everyone else, the baby crawls to a laptop on the floor and logs into an MTS account. After creating accounts on multiple social networking sites, it even goes on to broadcast a video before using the GPS system to navigate out of the hospital ward. The shocked receptionist is viewing a video of the baby on YouTube as the protagonist makes his exit. The commercial signs off with the text on the screen: 'Born for the internet. MTS 3GPlus Network.'

'Creativeland Asia' successfully combined cutting-edge graphics technology with exceptional visual storytelling.

Amitesh Rao, Director – Brand & Media, MTS India, elaborating on the campaign, said that the need was to reinforce the Unique Selling Proposition (USP). The fact that MTS 3GPlus network has been designed and optimised specifically for data; thereby being true to the MTS brand that talks of today's 24x7, always-on, data hungry consumer, for whom the internet is the biggest platform to avail opportunities.[7]

Sajan Raj Kurup, Founder and Creative Chairman, 'Creativeland Asia', the agency behind the campaign, speaking about the advertisement, said that the script for the film began with the simple insight that today's kids seem so comfortable with technology, devices and the internet, even as babies. The thought was pushed a little further; and after six months of 'painful labour', the baby is finally out.[8]

2. *Cadbury 5 Star*

Cadbury India had launched a multimedia campaign for its chocolate brand '5 Star'. The TVC, conceptualised by 'Ogilvy & Mather'company, went on air on 11 February.

'Cadbury India' steps out of the familiar 'Ramesh-Suresh' duo in the latest campaign for its '5 Star' brand. The advertisement pitches '5 Star' as the revolutionary new treatment for 'seriousness' which has become a social disease.

The advertisement traces the genesis of seriousness and how it assumed endemic proportions, before revealing '5 Star' as a solution in the typical style of a pharmaceutical advert, with a doctor demonstrating how the chocolate brand works on the body and brain to cure seriousness.

The advertisement opens with a voice-over saying that centuries ago children were born happy. It shows newly-born children laughing out loud. But one fine day, a dangerous disease changed everything and children were born 'serious'. The advertisement shows several children behaving seriously, like grown-ups. A doctor then introduces the cure to this problem – a bar of '5 Star'. The chocolate bar cures a grumpy boss and the advertisement ends with the line, 'Cadbury 5 Star *andar*, seriousness *bahar*' (Cadbury 5 Star inside; seriousness outside).

***Abhijit Avasthi*, national creative director, O&M**, said, that the communication in and around '5 Star' has been providing people with a sense of levity and lightness for many years. The campaign has been focussing on the 'Jo khaye kho jaaye' (Whoever eats, goes into oblivion) concept for the last eight to nine years; but now the brand wanted to move the bar a little higher by reaching out to youngsters.[10]

Woman related Advertising Laws in India

The Government of India has not set up a regulatory body in India to regulate advertisements. But as in due course depending on the nature of the grievances, the power to regulate advertisements may be exercised by a vast variety of authorities, including the courts, Central and state governments, tribunals or the police authorities. In addition to that, numerous legislations also deal with advertisement provisions in part, unfortunately, though not in total. (Refer Annexure - IV for the list of laws, rules and regulations that deal with advertisements.)

But, in the cases related to the rights of a woman, only the following laws/codes count:

1. ***The ASCI Code*:** Chapter – II states—Advertisements should contain nothing indecent, vulgar, especially in the depiction of women, or nothing repulsive which is likely, in the light of generally prevailing standards of decency and propriety, to cause grave and widespread offence.
2. ***Indecent Representation of Women (Prohibition) Act, 1986*:** The Act prohibits indecent representation of women through advertisements or in publications, writings, paintings, figures or in any other manner and for matters connected therewith or incidental thereto.
3. ***Cable Television Network Rules, 1994:*** Sub-point 6 of Rule 7 states—No advertisement shall be permitted which projects a derogatory image of women. (Refer Annexure - III)[11]
5. ***Doordarshan Commercial Code, 1987*:** Point 2 of the Code states—No advertisement shall be permitted which projects a derogatory image of women.
6. ***Press Council of India's Norms of journalistic conduct*:** Point 6 states—The Press shall not intrude or invade the right to privacy of an individual unless overridden by public interest.

Suggestions

The researcher, in her period of study on this topic, has found some serious defects in areas, not directly related to the topic of research.

The researcher sent electronic mails to seek the opinion of some of the most important NGOs working for the protection of the rights of woman; but, even after repeated reminders and requests, only a few bothered to reply to the query mentioned in the research question

The NGOs/Organisations that were contacted were:

Name of NGO	*Person to be contacted*	*Email id*	*Address*	*State*	*Remarks*
Joint Women's Programme	Dr.(Ms.)Jyotsna Chatterjee, Director	jwp@airtel mail.in	Flat 301, Shri Ram Residence Ahinsa Khand- 2 Indirapuram, Gaziabad	Delhi & NCR	No re-sponse
STOP	Ms. Roma De-babrata, President	romadeba@ vsnl.com	A – 25, Ground floor Chitranjan Park New Delhi-110 019	Delhi & NCR	No re-sponse
Apne Aap Women Worldwide	Ms. Ruchira Gupta, Executive Di-rector	ruchiragup ta@gmail. com	D-56, Anand Niketan	Delhi & NCR	Respond-ed
Human Rights Law Network	Mr. Colin Gon-salves Advocate	Colin.gon salves@hrln. org	576,Masjid Road Jungpura,New Delhi14	Delhi & NCR	No re-sponse
AIDWA	Ms.Sudha Sund-araman	aidwacec@ gmail.com	121,VP House Rafi Marg New Delhi	Delhi & NCR	No re-sponse
Action India	Gowri Choud-hury, Director	actionin dia1976@ gmail.com	National Secre-tariat PWDVA, 2005 C/o Action India 5/27A, Jangpu-ra-B New Delhi-14	Delhi & NCR	No re-sponse
The National Alliance of Women (NAWO)	Dr. Ruth Man-orama, President	Ruth. manorama@ gmail.com	U-9, IInd Floor, Green Park Extn, New Delhi - 110016	Delhi & NCR	No re-sponse

Centre for Feminist Legal Research	Ratna Kapoor, Director	cflr_45@yahoo.com	C/602,1st Floor New Friends Colony New Delhi- 110 065	Delhi & NCR	No response
Centre for Social Research	Ms. Ranjana Kumari, Director	ranjanakumari@csrindia.org	2,Institutional Area, Nelson Mandela Marg C-1 Vasant Kunj, New Delhi -70	Delhi & NCR	No response
Navjyoti India foundation	Dr. Kiran Bedi, Executive Director	admin@navjyoti.org.in	Khasra No. 99, Village Mohammadpur, Majri Karala, Near Sector- 22, Rohini Delhi - 110 081	Delhi & NCR	No response
SHAKTI VAHINI	Lokendra Kaushik, Coordinator	shaktivahini@yahoo.co.in	H-11, 2nd Floor, Hudson Lines, Kingsway Camp, New Delhi 110009	Delhi & NCR	No response
Maitri	Office	maitri.india@maitri.org.in	J-92 , Anant Ram Dairy Complex R K Puram, Sector- 13, INDIA New Delhi-110066	Delhi & NCR	No response
Smile Foundation	Meena Batra, Project Director	snehamumbai@snehamumbai.org	V-11, Green Park Ext New Delhi 110016	Delhi & NCR	No response
Sapna		ngo.sapna@gmail.com			No response
All India Women's Conference	Mrs. Veena Kohli, President	president@aiwc.org.in	Sarojini House, 6 Bhagwan Dass Road, New Delhi-11000	Delhi & NCR	No response
YWCA of India	Office	ywcaind@airtelmail.in	10, Parliament Street New Delhi-110001	Delhi & NCR	No response
Sakshi		connect@sakshingo.org	D-332 Defence Colony New Delhi 110024, India	Delhi & NCR	No response

Jagori	Abha Bhaiya Director	jagori@ jagori.org	B-114, Shivalik Malviya Nagar New-Delhi	Delhi & NCR	No re- sponse
Human Rights Law Network	Office	contact@ hrln.org	Human Rights Law Network c/o Socio-Legal Information Centre 576, Masjid Road, Jungpura New Delhi – 110014	Delhi & NCR	No re- sponse
Naz Foun- dation	Sangini	sangini97@ hotmail.com	Sangini (India) Trust, c/o Naz Foundation, PO Box 3910, An- drews Gunj, New Delhi 110049,	Delhi & NCR	No re- sponse
Swadhina	Srichandra Ven- kataramanan, Asst. Secretary	mainoffice. swadhina@ gmail.com	Swadhina 34/C Bondel Road, Ballygunge, Kolkata (Calcut- ta) 700019 India	Kolkata	Respond- ed

Of all the above NGOs contacted repeatedly over and over again, just two of them responded. One is 'Swadhina' of Kolkata and the other is 'Apne Aap Women Worldwide' of Delhi. The former is the only one from the above list that responded with genuine concern and interest; but, the latter (Apne Aap Women Worldwide) just responded in a single line, "I have not seen the ad so cannot comment." (Source: Personal interview by the researcher)

The finding of the researcher is rather shocking that most of these NGOs are just a shield for furthering their vested interests and nothing else. Had these NGOs been actually bothered about the state of violation of rights of woman, then, they would have definitely cared to reply.

'Asian Centre for Human Rights' (ACHR) report – 'India's Funds to NGOs Squandered' – released on 18 January 2013 alleged that the Union Government's funding to voluntary organisations was a scam and is in dire need of reform, as the audit by the Comptroller and Auditor-General of

India (CAG) was infrequent, inadequate and does not include the NGOs.[12] The report points out that as per replies received under the RTI Act, the Central Ministries and the State governments provided at least Rs. 6,654.35 crores as grants to NGOs and voluntary organisations between 2002-03 and 2008-09 — Rs. 4,757 crores by the Centre and Rs. 1,897 crores by the state.

ACHR Director Suhas Chakma noted, "The CAG report concluded that 7,916 fund utilisation certificates from the grantees for grant worth Rs. 96.79 crores from 1981-2009 were not obtained under the scheme of Grants-in-Aid for voluntary agencies. The CAG also noted that the possibility of misutilisation of funds or fraud cannot be ruled out, as majority of agencies who took grants neither came back to the National Afforestation & Eco-Development Board for the next instalment, after release of first instalment, nor did they furnish progress reports. From pre-funding assessment to evaluation of the activities implemented [by NGOs], there are no mechanisms. The funding given to NGOs is not subject to the CAG audit while the decision-making process of funding by the officials too has never been subject to any evaluation."[13]

Further another report shows the gross state of affairs in the state of NGOs in India. The Delhi high court has called for toughening of licensing norms for NGOs observing that 99% of them are 'fraud' and 'merely money making devices'. 'Most private run so called philanthropic organizations do not understand their social responsibilities. 99% of the existing NGOs are fraud and simply moneymaking devices. Only one out of every hundred NGOs serves the purpose they are set up for. There is a need for toughening of licensing norms and the legislature has to keep this in mind', a bench headed by Justice Pradeep Nandrajog said. The stinging remarks came, while the court was hearing a petition filed by two children homes viz. 'Chatravas' and 'Arya Orphanage' challenging government's refusal to grant them license under the Women and Children's Institutions (Licensing) Act, 1956 and dismissing their prayer for registration under the Juvenile Justice Act.

Some of the suggestions that the researcher would like to put forward are mentioned as follows:

1. It is an undisputed fact that advertisement plays a vital role in building up any business. The aim of advertisement is to attract the sales and enhance the visibility of the products and services of the company among the consumers. Through an advertisement, a company can build an image which it wants to make in the minds of the people. Therefore,

nowadays, companies spend a huge amount of their resources on advertising and promotional strategies. Thus, it is evident that, apart from ASCI, there are no specific legislations governing advertising in India. But, even ASCI is not up to the mark to govern over the advertising spectrum. It is evident that all that is needed is a codified uniform legislation as Advertising Laws.

2. We should also have laws like the Indecent Displays (Control) Act 1981 which is an Act of Parliament covering Scotland, England and Wales, but not Northern Ireland. It is concerned with preventing the display of 'indecent' material to the unsuspecting public. The Act does not define indecency, although it does give some directions as to how a display can be considered indecent. It establishes that 'if any indecent matter is publicly displayed, the person making the display and any person causing or permitting the display to be made, shall be guilty of an offence'.
3. We should also have laws like the Indecent Advertisements Prohibition Act, 1963; that is enforced in Bangladesh. It defines:
   (a) 'advertisement' includes any notice, circular or other document, displayed on any house, building or wall, or published in any newspaper or periodical, and any announcement made orally or by any means of producing or transmitting light or sound, but does not include trade circulars issued by manufacturers of drugs to medical practitioners.
   (b) 'indecent' includes whatsoever that may amount to any incentive to sensuality and excitement of impure thoughts in the mind of an ordinary man of normal temperament, and has the tendency to deprave and corrupt those whose minds are open to such immoral influence, and which is deemed to be detrimental to public morals and calculated to produce pernicious effect, in depraving and debauching the minds of persons.
4. We should have such laws that are binding on both the producers and advertisers of the products. Unless the laws are strict, advertisers will not be cautious regarding their violations of other's rights.
5. It is also the duty of the aware citizens and institutions like judiciary to raise their voice through Public Interest Litigations against airing of such advertisements on national television.
6. Under the Cable Television Networks (Regulation) Act, the ministry issues directions to television channels or cable TV operators to stop airing an advertisement and not to the advertisers. But

unless the advertisers are booked and given penalty, the menace of such advertisements would be seem more than often in national television.

7. Philanthropic institutions should understand their duties and responsibilities well and should go out to all minimum extent to protect the weak and the vulnerable sections of the society for which they are set up. These organizations should not shy away from their responsibilities.

Conclusion

As for the MTS campaign, there are many things that they did right. The advertisement has used cutting-edge graphics technology to make the baby look real. It has done a great job in creating a baby with such detailed qualities and emotions. The advertisement is based on the simple insight that today's kids are very comfortable with technology and the internet. The way they released the advertisement on a Bit Torrent site, the way they created the social content around 'FourSquare' and 'Twitter', the way they tried to seed the commercial first with the internet generation. To me, that is where the good things of the commercial ends. The TVC, by itself, is not that path breaking. There is no reason to push commercial messages through babies (even if it is a white baby for brown parents) at a certain level. It even contravenes the self-regulation guidelines that many advertisers have started to use. However, the whole idea that kids use technology in a way as if they were born with it, has been taken way too seriously by the brand. Some of the instances, where the baby cuts his umbilical cord through the help of 'Google Search' and the use of navigation seem a bit too exaggerated. Though, it is an endearing effort by the brand and the advertisement has surely garnered a huge response in the highly cluttered telecom category, but, the question remains whether the delivery process of the child should have been a part of the advertisement.

The Delhi High Court on April 1, 2014 stayed the order of the 'Advertising Standards Council of India' that asked 'Sistema Shyam Teleservices Ltd' not to air after April 7, 2014 an advertisement which the company claims to depict the speed of its Internet service. Justice Manmohan stayed ASCI's March 24, 2014 decision, holding the advertisement's contents as 'gross and indecent' and 'offensive especially to women'. Central government's standing counsel Neeraj Chaudhari told the court that the Ministry of Information and Broadcasting had not passed any direction to give effect to ASCI's order. He said that under the Cable Television Networks (Regulation) Act, the ministry issues directions to television channels or cable TV operators to stop airing an advertisement and not to the advertisers.

As for the 'Cadbury 5 Star' campaign, it is based on a powerful insight that people have become too serious in life. They should rather be free of pressure and shrug off the seriousness that follows them everywhere. The campaign uses 'humour and comic relief' to cure this disease, i.e. plaguing everyone. The advertisement uses characters that are noticeable and will attract the consumer's attention. The advertisement ends very well when the doctor shoves a bar of '5-Star' (chocolate) like an injection down the grumpy boss' throat to cure his seriousness. It is a well-executed advertisement that will garner eyeballs. The tagline – 'Cadbury 5 Star *andar*, seriousness *bahar*' – is interesting. However, it is difficult to understand how 'Cadbury 5 Star' can help get rid of seriousness. Also, the film is packed with so much that it takes more than a couple of viewings to get the message. The visual device of using grown up faces on baby bodies is something that people might find hard to comprehend. On the flip side, the product section is absolutely smashing. Compared to Ramesh-Suresh, this campaign requires a bit of figuring out as the storyline is more complex."

A positive and the good way to look at it, is through the words of Prof. Avinash Mantri (Brand Consultant and Faculty in Advertising and Brand Management, SIES College, Navi Mumbai) who says, "It is not at all the violation of the rights to privacy of a woman. It is one of nature's most beautiful moments- giving birth. More sleazy acts like cameras irrelevantly focussing on private parts and general skin show don't raise an outcry from women groups and are beamed into living rooms of families." (*Source*: Personal interview by the Researcher)

The researcher would like to conclude with the words of Ms. Srichandra Venkataramanan, Asst. Secretary at 'Swadhina' (a voluntary organisation for woman and children based in Kolkata) who says:

"There is no doubt about the fact that showing child birth is a gross violation of the privacy rights of women. Child-birth is a scientific as well as a private moment for any woman - that is one reason why even in the remotest areas where delivery is done at home or during accidental deliveries during travel, the first action that is taken is to create a barrier surrounding the woman with the help of whatever that is available around.

Though we agree that the child-birth depicted in the advertisements or movies, is an enacted situation, but, often it dilutes the importance of child-birth itself by making it appear as a fun situation (case in point is the MTS advertisement). Another thing which is often overlooked is the impact of the advertisements on children. Any child today knows that babies are born through the mothers, but, most children below the puberty age have no idea about how a child is delivered. So, openly depicting a child-birth, provides them only confusing ideas and arouses more and more questions in their mind. It is also highly embarrassing for a mother to watch the advertisement with her child. Such depictions take away the sanctity associated with child-birth and exposes the most private moment of a woman's life." (*Source*: Personal interview by the Researcher)

References

1 P. Pathak, J. (2014). Portrayal of child delivery in Indian TV Advertisements vis-à-vis Right to Privacy of Women. *IOSR Journal of Humanities and Social Science, 19*(5), 06-14. doi:10.9790 /0837-19530614

2 Pathak, J. P. (2014). *Introduction to Media Laws and Ethics*. Delhi: Shipra Publications.

3 Advertising, Marketing, Media, Digital, PR News & more | Campaign India. (n.d.). Retrieved from http://www.campaignindia.in

4 *Come 26th March, 2014 - Babies In India Will Be 'Born For The Internet'*. (n.d.). Retrieved from https://www.mtsindia.in/corporate/downloads/Come%20 26th%20March,%202014%20-%20Babies%20In%20India%20Will%20 Be%20'Born%20For%20The%20Internet'.pdf

5 MTS India - MTS MBlaze, MTS CDMA India, MTS MBrowse, MTS CDMA SmartPhone, MTS Android Phones. (n.d.). Retrieved from http://www. mtsindia.in/

6 MTS targets 'net gen' again, with an 'internet baby' | Advertising | Campaign India. (n.d.). Retrieved from http://www.campaignindia.in/video/mts-targets-net-gen-again-with-an-internet-baby/420369

7 *MTS gives birth to an internet baby*. (n.d.). Retrieved from http://www. exchange4media.com/advertising/mts-gives-birth-to-an-internet-baby_54848.html

8 *Creativeland Asia eyes the bigger picture*. (n.d.). Retrieved from http:// www.campaignindia.in/article/creativeland-asia-eyes-the-bigger-picture/423199

9 *Cadbury 5Star promises to 'cure' seriousness*. (n.d.). Retrieved from http://www.campaign india. in /video/cadbury-5star-promises-to-cure-seriousness/420293

10 *Why so serious? Cadbury 5 Star offers the perfect cure in latest ad.* (n.d.). Retrieved from http://www.exchange4media.com/advertising/why-so-serious-cadbury-5-star-offers-the-perfect-cure-in-latest-ad_54675.html

11 *Programme and Advertising Codes prescribed under the Cable Television Network Rules, 1994.* Retrieved from http://cablequest.org/pdfs/i_b/programme-advt-code.pdf

12 *'A huge scam running into crores' - New Delhi - The Hindu.* (n.d.). Retrieved from http://www.thehindu.com/todays-paper/tp-national/tp-newdelhi/a-huge-scam-running-into-crores/article4330537.ece

13 *'99 ngos are fraud money-making devices: HC'* - New Delhi -*Hindustan Times.* (n.d.). Retrieved from http://www.hindustantimes.com/india-news/newdelhi/99-ngos-are-fraud-money-making-devices-hc/article1-1021701.aspx

5

Advertising Vis-A-Vis Human Rights

Lasciviousness

Media, being the fourth pillar of democracy, is supposed to behave in a responsible and ethical way. Therefore, it is the obligation of the advertisers not to come up with advertisements which misguide, mislead, misinform the consumers or offend good public taste.[1]

Unfortunately, there have been instances where Indian advertisers have come up with certain advertisements which have shocked public conscience and have subsequently been banned on the grounds of public decency or morality.

Decency in advertisements invokes the concept of 'media ethics' which aims at making the advertisers responsible by infusing the aspect of 'morality' into the advertising sector. The need to curb obscenity in advertising also finds its justification in the jurisprudential doctrine of 'parens patraie' which means that the state should act as a parent of its subjects and ensure their best interests.[2]

1. ***Calida Underwear; 1990s:*** Here, Dino Moreo is seen tugging Bipasha Basu's underwear with his teeth. The then Minister of State for Cultural affairs, Mr Anil Deshmukh found the advertisement a little hard to handle and for obvious reasons it was added to the long list of 'Banned Indian Commercials'. The tag line- 'And you thought your appetite for indulgence could only be whetted by Swiss chocolates', added the right amount of fuel to the fire.
2. ***Kamasutra Condoms; Early 1990s:*** The steamy commercial featuring Pooja Bedi's seductive shower that attracts Marc Robinson was instantly banned and prohibited from transmission by the Indian legal authorities.
3. ***Mr. Coffee; Early 1990s:*** This advertisement featuring Mallaika and Arbaaz tried to portray the concept of good coffee, but the commercial was not very well understood by the Indian legal authorities. The tagline, 'Real pleasure can't come in an instant', and the commercial, due to its sexual overtones generated quite a controversy in the early 90's.

4. ***Tuff Shoes; 1995:*** In 1995, when Milind Soman and Madhu Sapre posed nude for the Tuff Shoes Ad campaign, they probably never saw a fourteen year-long court case ahead of them. Two pairs of shoes, a python and two nude models got various women's groups fuming, the models slapped with a case of obscenity and the advertisement deemed unfit for public consumption. Fourteen years later in 2009, the models and the others involved were finally acquitted and all charges against them dropped.[2]
5. ***New York Lotto; Year: 1999:*** This advertisement surfaced out of nowhere in 2010 to create some controversy as actor Bipasha Basu is seen topless in this advertisement from the 90's. Bipasha had done this commercial in 1999, when she was modelling for 'Ford Modelling Agency' in New York.
6. ***Moods Condom; 2000s:*** Riding with her boyfriend on a bike, the girl is turned on just by the thought of the product. The advertisement is seen with the girl touching, fondling and biting him; making the content unfit for public consumption.
7. ***Levis; 2000s:*** The hot and hunky Akshay Kumar is dressed in a pair of jeans and showing off his perfect abs. The female model is all out to seduce him and then unbuttons his jeans. [2,3]
8. ***Zatak Talc; 2000s:*** The female model, who goes to give her measurement to a tailor, gets turned on by him when she realises him wearing the advertised product.[2,6] The expression and gestures of the female model makes the advertisement unfit for public viewing.
9. ***Maxima Waterproof Watch; 2000s:*** The advertisement features a girl fantasizing about seducing a man. She ties him to the bed, kissing and seducing him. However, before audience starts expecting a lot more action, it ends with a woman stealing the watch and walking away.
10. ***Slice; 2000s:*** Katrina Kaif's commercial of 'Slice' became quite famous because of her subtle seductive act in the advertisement. This commercial is widely known as the 'Aamsutra' and portrays the actress in a sensual avatar licking the drink from her fingertips.
11. ***Denver deodorant; 2000s:*** A bikini clad model gets turned on by a male staring at her just because he has put on the advertised deodorant.[2,4] She gets so turned on that she is willing to undress herself on the beach itself. The expressions and the model's seduction act make the ***commercial lascivious.***
12. ***Bisleri - Play Safe; 2001:*** In 2000, Bisleri shifted from 'Pure and Safe' to 'Play safe' in 2000 to target the youth and convey a social message. The

company felt the shift had been necessitated by the fact that every new entrant in the mineral water market adopted the purity mantra. The idea certainly differentiated Bisleri from other brands but the woman, the beach, the man and the whole hidden idea of 'safe sex' didn't quite sell well and the advertisement, as most would have expected, was banned.[5]

13. ***Levis - Low Rise jeans; 2001:*** Levis has always positioned itself as a 'youth' brand and with this advertisement they had proved that the concept of sex sells.[2] The lascivious factor exhibited by the sexy women in the ad was mainly targeted at women who wanted to look more erotic and sexy. The commercial was not banned but the almost semi-naked women in it did manage to create quite a controversy for the commercial makers.
14. ***AC Black Whisky - Kuch Bhi Ho Sakta Hai; 2002:*** 'AC Black Whisky' stirred up a controversy when, during the World Cup, this advertisement was aired at regular intervals. The commercial featured a woman with her neckline diminishing and a man with his shirt coming off together with the tagline 'Kuch Bhi ho sakta hai' (Anything can happen). The commercial was instantly banned.[2,6]
15. ***Amul Macho Undergarments; 2007:*** This advertisement was banned by the 'Advertising Standards Council of India'. The advertisement with the tagline 'Ye to bada toing hai' (suggesting sex appeal) is rated as one of the most vulgar and sexually explicit advertisements in the history of Indian advertising. This advertisement, although banned, increased the market share of the company sharply with a turnover of Rs. 201 crores in 2007-2008.[7]
16. ***Wild Stone Deodorant; 2007*:** The advertisement, shot during Durga Pooja, depicts how a homely Bengali lady bumps into a hot man wearing the advertised product; and that the fragrance takes them into a fantasy world. The commercial justified the tagline 'Wild by Nature' and although, it was not banned, a highly censored version was aired on television.
17. ***Lux Cozy; 2007*:** A hot man clad in the advertised product is seen chasing a dog who pulled away his towel and then a scantily dressed woman comes up to him and gives him a peck on his cheek and thanks him for finding her dog. Then she walks away with a naughty look at the boy. The advertisement ends with the tagline 'Apna Luck Pehen he Chalo' (Wear your luck).[8] The Ministry of Information and Broadcasting banned transmission or re-transmission of the advertisement on the grounds of being indecent, vulgar and suggestive.

18. ***VIP Frenchie x Underwear; 2008:*** The advertisement features a trekking expedition of a young couple along with campfire and some playful games in the bedroom. The boy is then shown walking out of the bathroom in his underwear and the advertisement ends with the couple cosying up with the VIP X logo appearing on screen. The commercial is yet another instance of trying to portray lasciviousness as a mantra to sell a product.[9]
19. ***Manforce condom; 2012*:** The advertisement featured actor Sunny Leone posing seductively and showing off her cleavage. In the advertisement, she holds her outfit with one hand and reaches for black grapes with the other.[10]

Laws Regulating Obscenity in Advertisements in India:

1. ***The Indian Penal Code, 1860*:** India has a quite a few legislations to govern various aspects of advertisements. As far as the obscenity is concerned, Section 292 of the Indian Penal Code, 1860 is the over-arching law which makes it a punishable offence to publish, distribute, sell, hire or circulate any obscene material, which thereby makes punishable the obscenity displayed in advertisements. The more narrowed down legal framework pertaining to the advertisements is given in 'Cable Television Networks Rules 1994' and the 'Advertising Standards Council of India' (ASCI) Code.
2. ***Cable television networks rules, 1994***[11] **:** Section 6 of the Rules state—It provides that no programme (including advertisement) which has the likelihood of offending good taste or decency should be aired on the television.
3. ***Advertising Standards Council of India (ASCI):*** Apart from this, the 'Advertising Standards Council of India' (ASCI), which is a powerful self-regulatory organization for the advertising industry, in its 'Code for Self-Regulation in Advertising' stipulates that advertisements should not be offensive to the generally accepted standards of public decency and should not contain anything indecent, vulgar or repulsive.
4. ***The Indecent Representation of Women Prohibition Act, 1987:*** In addition to these laws, the Indecent Representation of Women Prohibition Act, 1987 also puts an embargo on any kind of indecent representation of women in advertisements, in any form whatsoever.

Analysis

In July 2007, two vulgar advertisements were taken off air.[2] The Information and Broadcasting Ministry has banned television advertisements of two underwear brands on grounds that they are in 'bad taste'. The ban came immediately after the Ministry released a draft-code for self-regulating the broadcast content on television channels. The government imposing ban on the two 'obscene' commercials—the underwear advertisements by 'Lux Cozy' and another by 'Amul Macho'—had raised questions whether the advertising industry is guilty of making indecent advertisements. Josy Paul (National Creative Director, JWT advertising agency), Bharat Patel (Consultant, Advertising Standard Council of India) and Akhila Sivadasa (Executive director, Centre for Advocacy and Research) debated the issue on CNN-IBN show 'Face the Nation'.

The following can be deduced from the summary of the interview:

It is unfair to slam the advertising industry for the indecent advertisements as it is the very same industry that has produced famous slogans like 'Hamara Bajaj' and churned out great advertisements like that of adhesive brand 'Fevicol'. Interestingly, the two banned advertisements were reviewed and okayed by the 'Advertising Standards Council of India'—a self-regulatory body that regulates advertisements and ensures the content of the commercials are not unethical, obscene, derogatory, misleading or in poor taste. The body received complaints from consumer groups, acting upon which, in March 2007, ASCI had asked the advertisers to modify the advertisements. However, despite the modification, it kept getting complaints from viewers who said that the 'Amul Macho' commercial was 'vulgar' and unfit for family viewing. The advertisement was modified by the advertisers; but, still, the ASCI and the Information and Broadcasting Ministry kept receiving complaints on the advertisement which led the government to finally call for a ban. The advertisement is offensive as it not only carries a sexual connotation; but, to watch a woman wash male underwear in itself, is derogatory and reiteration of stereotypes. ASCI can regulate and ban commercials on grounds of obscenity. However it doesn't have a code to stop advertisements that portray women in a derogatory light.

Josy Paul, who had worked on one of the above mentioned two commercials, admitted in the show, 'Face the Nation', that he himself was not too happy to be associated with its meaning. The creative director—one who conceptualises the advertisement—faces extreme pressure from the marketing departments and the brands to make TVC titillating enough for it to 'stand out' in the crowd.

There are four Cs in the advertising industry —client, consumer, channel and the creative agency. These four things together create an advertisement. Thus, it is the collective responsibility of the client, the consumer, the channel and the creative agency to ensure that an immoral, derogatory, objectionable material does not go out.

Incidentally, both the advertisements in question carry popular brands names—'Amul' and 'Lux'—that are also the registered brand names of two separate, bigger companies 'Amul' (milk products) and 'Lux' (soaps). Perhaps the government should do something about misleading trademarks as well.

It seems that the arguments advocating the preposition that more stringent checks on obscenity in advertisements hold more weight than the counter-arguments for the same. If one looks at advertisements, they do, in fact, have universal viewership and are not meant for a particular segment of society. On the contrary, films are governed by the Cinematograph Act 1952; wherein their viewership can be regulated by dividing their public exhibition into four classes viz. Unrestricted Public exhibition, Unrestricted Public exhibition under parental guidance, Public exhibition restricted to adults and Public exhibition restricted to a special class of person by certifying them as U, UA, A and S respectively. In light of such a wide viewership base in the case of advertisements, we need stricter measures to curb obscenity in cases of advertisements so that these can be viewed by everyone. Apart from this, the fact that advertisements force themselves into the viewers by virtue of being broadcast as a package deal further ensures that everyone watches it.

This can be contrasted as against films where the aspect of 'voluntariness' is not absent and the person has to make certain efforts to get access to the film. As viewing advertisements is not a voluntary decision made and it comes along when one watches television, the content should be regulated in such a way that it does not offend public taste and is suitable of being viewed by everyone.

The argument that there is a lack of evidence to prove that such advertisements do not have an effect upon tender young minds is totally devoid of merit. There have been numerous studies which prove that television advertisements have influenced children in various ways, for instance, to demand for advertised products etc. Not only children, but also the huge rural masses that are still uneducated would not be in a position to appreciate any sort of sexual references displayed in the advertisements.

Thus, children and illiterate people would be worst affected if obscene advertisements are displayed very openly on television, which warrants a stricter check on obscenity in advertisements.

Lastly, the problem that there is a lack of agreement on what is tantamount to 'obscenity' in advertisements cannot be an excuse to leave this domain of law unregulated.

Suggestions

1. It should be the collective responsibility of the client, the consumer, the channel and the creative agency to ensure that an immoral, derogatory, objectionable material does not go out.
2. ASCI should be made a stronger body by vesting in it certain statutory powers. Considering that seventy-five percent of the advertising sector is regulated by ASCI as well as the fact that the 'Cable Television Networks (Amendment) Rules, 2006' stipulates that all the advertisements will have to abide by ASCI's Code for 'Self-Regulation in Advertising', it seems that ASCI is the body which should regulate obscenity in Indian advertisements in future as well. It is suggested that ASCI should, in fact, be given certain binding powers, however, it does not mean that ASCI would be elevated to the position of state.
2. ASCI should also be given the power to screen the advertisements before they are aired on television, so that the advertisements offending good public taste are not broadcast at the first place.
3. Apart from this, there should be a robust mechanism which deters the advertisers to air obscene advertisements. ASCI should be conferred the power to impose binding financial sanctions, the amount of which should be reasonably high to deter various advertisers and advertising agencies.
4. However, there is a possibility that those big advertisers and advertising agencies which annually earn huge amount of profit would easily bypass such a system of financial sanctions and would keep airing obscene advertisements. To check such advertisers, the ASCI should be linked with criminal courts which can impose criminal sanctions on such advertisers showing recurring obscenity in their advertisements. There should be a swift linkage between ASCI and courts, wherein the former can take the blameworthy advertisers to the courts and get them punished.
5. It is suggested that not only the advertisers who come up with obscene advertisements, but also the television channels which screen such advertisements should be deemed culpable and be subsequently punished. If such suggestions are taken into account and ASCI is made

a stronger body, we can regulate the television advertisements thereby substantially curbing the ill-effects of obscene advertising in the Indian society.

6. Lastly, it is suggested that even if obscenity is an extremely vague and subjective concept, the yardstick of a 'reasonable man' should be used to deal with determination of obscenity in advertisements.

Conclusions

"I do not regard advertising as entertainment or an art form, but as a medium of information" quoted David Ogilvy.[12] Ogilvy's famous quote emphasising on the utility of an advertisement seems redundant whilst considering the current scenario of the advertising industry.

Advertising, in its essence, should be a means of communicating information and not as a means of expressing the creative ability of the advertiser. Advertising agencies have realised that the attention span of consumers can be tapped by introducing a mix of obscurity and sensationalism in their endeavours. The sphere of product publicity has bourgeoned from a seemingly monotonous print intimation to an elaborate chain of television advertisements and promotional ventures. The advertising industry today tries to catch the attention and compel the buyer to agree to the superiority of the product they are endorsing.

Due to the free hand that the advertisers and consumers enjoy on this medium, misleading and vulgar advertisements are aplenty and exaggerating the capabilities of a product to lure users to procurement is an established fact. It is not that the misleading commercials have restricted themselves to the virtual domain, television media has been consistently targeting for airing the most dubious advertisements regardless of their repercussions. The Indian advertising industry is heavily criticised for airing incongruous advertisements for the sole motive of inducing interest in the product. Such acts have resulted in a sense of disgust which the viewing public has developed over the years of continuous exposure to such content. Finally it can be concluded that quality product with witty advertising will always be far more effective than the ones with vulgarity.

References

1 *Obscenity In Television Advertisements: Do we need more stringent measures of scrutiny than used in films?*. (n.d.). Retrieved from http://www.legalera.in/interviews/item/7082-obscenity-in-television-advertisements-do-we-need-more-stringent-measures-of-scrutiny-than-used-in-films

2 Pathak, J. P. (2015). Portrayal of Lasciviousness; an Analysis of Indian TV Ads. Retrieved from http://iosrjournals.org/iosr-jhss/papers/Vol20-issue4/Version-6/C020462028.pdf

3 *Ghost of Bipasha's Past (Bipasha Basu Topless).* (n.d.). Retrieved from https://www.youtube.com/watch?v=DV_x_DZyVbs

4 *The Advertisements that almost said it 'All'.* (n.d.). Retrieved from http://english.kolkata24x7.com/lifestyle/the-advertisements-that-almost-said-it-all

5 *Reinventing Bisleri.* (n.d.). Retrieved from http://www.icmrindia.org/free%20resources/casestudies/reinventing-bisleri2.htm

6 *YouTube- AC Black - Kuch Bhi Ho Sakta Hai.mp4.* (n.d.). Retrieved from https://www.youtube.com/watch?v=XBd_n_VO8Nc

7 *Banned Commercials or ads in india: Amul Macho Undergarments.* (n.d.). Retrieved from http://bannedcommercialsinindia.blogspot.in/2013/03/AmulMacho.html

8 *Banned Commercials or ads in india.* (n.d.). Retrieved from http://bannedcommercialsinindia.blogspot.in/

9 *15 Indian Print & Television Advertisements That Courted Controversy.* (n.d.). Retrieved from https://www.scoopwhoop.com/inothernews/indian-advertisements-controversies/#.1r4jscxkn

10 *Top 5 Sexual and Sensual Indian Ads (WIldstone, KS, Maaza, Amul Macho, Manforce).* (n.d.). Retrieved from https://www.youtube.com/watch?v=DNnEBVn_ZOU

11 *The Cable Television Networks Rules, 1994.* (n.d.). Retrieved from http://www.wipo.int /edocs/lexdocs/laws/en/in/in079en.pdf

12 Singh, M. P. (2007). *Quote Unquote A Handbook of Famous Quotations.* Lotus Books.

6

Advertising Vis-A-Vis Human Rights

Colour Discrimination

Discrimination based on skin colour, or colourism, is a form of prejudice or discrimination in which human beings are treated differently based on the social meanings attached to skin colour.[1]

Colourism, a term coined by Alice Walker in 1982, is not a synonym of racism.[2] 'Race' depends on multiple factors (including ancestry); therefore, racial categorization does not solely rely on skin colour.

Colourism can be found specifically in parts of Africa, Southeast Asia, East Asia, India, Latin America, and the United States. The abundance of colourism is a result of the global prevalence of 'pigmentocracy', a term recently adopted by social scientists to describe societies in which wealth and social status are determined by skin colour. Throughout the numerous pigmentocracies across the world, the lightest-skinned people have the highest social status, followed by the brown-skinned, and finally the black-skinned who are at the bottom of the social hierarchy. This form of prejudice often results in reduced opportunities for those who are discriminated against on the basis of skin colour; particularly, when the notion of whiteness is strongly associated with elements of 'purity' and 'fairness' while blackness is more allied to 'dirt' and 'evil'.

By the word 'colour discrimination' the researcher does not talk about the 'apartheid' problem but the study aims to focus on the prejudice behind the uneven skin tones of people belonging to the same country, that is, India.

In print, online and electronic media we often come across dominant messages that advertising companies are sending to people. The main purpose of the advertisers is to promote their products by conveying a message through these advertisements. Nowadays, it has been observed that advertisers exploit the concept of 'colourism' to advertise their products. According to these advertisements, fair skinned people tend to have higher social standing, more positive networks, and more opportunities to succeed than those of people with darker skin tones.

However, colour as a ground for discrimination is prohibited in the equality clause of the constitution of Bangladesh through Article 28(1)[3]. Although constitution only talks about discrimination based on religion, race, caste, sex or place of birth, but colour is conventionally grouped with race when unfair discrimination is in question (Article 1 of the International Convention on the Elimination of All Forms of Racial Discrimination). Moreover, international instruments also prohibited the discrimination based on any specific colour, such as Article 2 of 'Universal Declaration of Human Rights' (UDHR) and 'International Covenant on Civil and Political Rights' (ICCPR); and Article 14 of 'European Court of Human Rights' (ECHR).

The Roots of our Fair Obsession –The Indian Scenario

'Yashomati maiyya se bole Nand lala, Radha kyun gori, main kyun kala' (Lord Krishna asks Yashomati mother why am I dark but Radha fair?) — a devotional song has a tiny Lord Krishna beseeching his foster mother to find out why his lady love is fair while he is dark.[4] Much before, India was invaded by fair skinned people, and the country has been fascinated by the lighter colour of skin. In Sanskrit, the term 'Asuryasparsh' is used to define one, who is untanned, untouched by the sun's heat and is therefore pure and affluent.

In 1919, India got its first commercial fairness cream in 'Afghan Snow', manufactured by ES Patanwala, a perfumer/entrepreneur who came to Mumbai from a small principality (Jhalra Patan) in Rajasthan. The cream was named after King Zahir of Afghanistan as it reminded him of the snow from his homeland.

Hindustan Unilever (then Hindustan Levers) introduced a fairness cream in 1975 that was soft on skin unlike the bleaching creams of the time, usurping the fairness bleach market. Soon, they attained a pioneer status in the business.

Post liberalisation, a flurry of brands decided to get their hands white. It started with 'Emami Naturally Fair Herbal Fairness Cream' in the early 90s; CavinKare's 'Fairever' in 1998 and Godrej's 'FairGlow' in 1999. 'Emami' focussed on pearl extracts, 'FairGlow' on the 'no compromise with fair skin' positioning whereas 'Fairever', that went on to be the biggest challenger brand to 'Fair & Lovely' centred its advertising on its two unique ingredients — saffron and milk. Several brands that didn't bother themselves with fairness as a platform now have at least one and sometimes multiple variants addressing this need — for instance 'Garnier' and 'Lakme'.

The recent introduction of a fairness cream for a rather intimate part of female anatomy proves that marketeers are not even close to being done exploiting this category.

'Emami' was the first to leverage that men needed a fairness cream that suited their skin. It launched Fair & Handsome in 2005.

There are plenty of small fish in the fairness pond. Most of them are prevalent in markets like Uttar Pradesh and Madhya Pradesh. Some of these players are 'Neha & Love', 'Lufina', 'Melas', 'Toni N Lovely', 'Zohra and Roopa'.

In the year 2000, Dr R K Pandhi, then HOD of AIIMS Delhi's Dermatology department made an official statement to the press saying that none of the fairness creams have any valuable substantiation to their claims.

Protests against the fascination for fairer skin, and how it is adversely affecting the psyche of the Indian women, have been gaining ground, especially over social media. A non-profit organisation called 'Women of Worth' launched a campaign in 2009 called 'Dark is Beautiful'. Actor and activist Nandita Das became the face of the campaign.

An entire segment in Madhur Bhandarkar's 'Traffic Signal' is devoted to an anti lightness-cream rant.

'The Advertising Standards Council of India', a self-regulatory body has proposed a draft of new guidelines that tells skin lightening advertisements not to show darker skinned people as unhappy, depressed, or disadvantaged in any way by skin tone, and should not associate skin colour with any particular socioeconomic class, ethnicity or community. According to Sam Balsara, a former chairman of ASCI, "The reason for these guidelines is to make it clear to advertisers as to what society finds acceptable and what it doesn't."

Case Studies

For years, advertisers of skin-lightening creams and other products have shown people — mostly women — with dark skin as having problems when it comes to finding jobs, getting married and generally being accepted by society. The makers of these advertisements include behemoths like 'Unilever', 'Johnson & Johnson' and 'Procter & Gamble'. The so-called 'fairness' cream industry in India was estimated at $432 million a year and is growing by 18 per cent annually in 2010, according to AC Nielsen.[6] The researcher would be discussing about a few prominent case studies of advertisements which portray colour discrimination on national television in India.

1. ***Pond's White Beauty** (old ad)*: In 2008, 'Pond's' came up with a 5-part 45 second series, narrating a story of love, heartbreak and triumph. Saif Ali Khan breaks up with Priyanka Chopra who is clearly low on self-esteem. Priyanka starts using 'Pond's White Beauty' and gradually her superior pigmentation brings back both her confidence and the boy who abandons his fair love interest, Neha Dhupia.
2. ***Pond's White Beauty** (new ad):* Bollywood actor, Ileana D'cruz is the face for the new range in India. The product is 'New Pond's White Beauty Daily Anti-Spot Fairness Cream' to get spot-less radiant skin and reduce spots and dark circles to reveal a glowing skin.
3. ***Pond's white beauty BB+ foundation and fairness cream***: The target of the new 'Pond's white beautyTM BB+ Foundation and Fairness cream' is to make every girl look her 'selfie' best. The product, through its advertisement, vouches to be a girl's best friend when it comes to taking the perfect 'selfie'.
4. ***Pond's men oil control fairness moisturiser***: The advertisement of this moisturizer vouches its benefits for oily skin emphasizing on its potent, yet natural ingredients, which give best fairness results, in addition to reducing oiliness of the skin and tightening the skin pores temporarily.
5. ***Fair & Lovely***: A retired father is shown lamenting the absence of a son to bail him out of his financial limitations. His dark-skinned daughter decides to be the son; and uses a 'Fair & Lovely' to have a coveted job of a flight attendant. The brand promises the benefit of 'making complexion fairer over a period of six weeks'.
6. ***Fair & Lovely MAX Fairness for Men***:The current cream has specifications like affordable amount to be paid, works intensively on tough male skin, helps you have visible fairness in a couple of weeks, visible spot reduction and triple sunscreen UV protection.
7. ***Fair & Handsome***: This advertisement features Shahrukh Khan, who is seen recalling his past in a fictional representation when he was a regular guy who wanted to be a celebrity.
8. ***Clean & Dry***: This recent advertisement for 'Clean & Dry' emphasized that bleaching of the private parts would make the wife more adorable to the husband.
9. ***Garnier***: This advertisement features John Abraham who doesn't care as much about the dangerous effects of sun exposure as much as he does about tan lines on his bulging biceps.

10. ***Glam up Cream***: The girl says, "Aaj Rahul ke sath date hai…naya 'Glam up' jab dikhna ho special" (There's a date today with Rahul... New 'Glam Up' to look special).
11. ***Vaseline Men Anti-spot Whitening Total Fairness Serum***: The advertisement of the cream vouches that it ensures that the users have white and glowing skin, keeping them look younger for longer and protects their skin from harmful rays of sun.
12. ***Olay Natural White Healthy Fairness Night Cream***: The advertisement vouches that the cream is a combination of skin whitener, spot remover, and intense moisturizer that has the capacity to reveal healthy and radiant skin.
13. ***Olay White Radiance UV Whitening Day Cream***: The advertisement says that the product minimizes the skin pores and has advanced light diffusion technology and triple efficacy whitening formula.
14. ***Vaseline Healthy White UV Lightening Lotion***: The advertisement comes with promises of ensuring great skincare as the product is clinically proven for radiant, naturally lighter skin in only two weeks. The product comes with triple sunscreen for preventing further darkening, yogurt serum to moisturize the skin and active whitening system, including vitamin B3, that helps bring out naturally fair skin.
15. ***Garnier White Complete Fairness Cream***: The TVC shows one girl asking the other if she is happy with the fairness cream she uses. The latter replies in affirmative, as that she has always been using the product, thereby rating it 6 or 7 out of 10. The former asks her to change her cream immediately; and when asked for one reason, the former states ten reasons. The voiceover goes, 'Ab payiye 10 on 10 fairness naya Garnier White complete ke saath' (Now get 10 on 10 fairness with new Garnier White complete). And adds that its new technology that provides the user with ten benefits: instant whitening, sun protection SPF 17, long lasting fairness, glow, even skin tone, fresh skin, moisturised skin, smooth skin, anti-dark spots and healthy looking skin.
16. ***Garnier for Men PowerLight Intensive Fairness Face Wash & Cream***: The product ensures that it deep cleanses impurities & pollutants, helps eliminate dark skin cells, refreshes skin's glow naturally and has lemon extract & anti-oxidant grape water included.
17. ***Nivea advanced whitening oil control moisturizer***: This light and fast acting cream claims to give very fast results, with its sun protection action as well as moisturizing quality, to give a fair glowing skin in just a few weeks.

18. ***Boroplus body lotion***: Kareena Kapoor endorses the product and advocates its skin lightening qualities. 'Boroplus Healthy & Fair Winter Cream' addresses the need of fairness cream users who find their creams inadequate to battle dry skin brought on by winter. This cream combines the promise of fairness along with winter protection.
19. ***Nutregena Fine Fairness cream:*** Another TVC promoting 'skin whitening' is 'Neutrogena Fine Fairness Cream', which claims to give fair skin by reducing the effect of melanin, and at the same time accelerated cell renewal process for best results. Additionally, this skin cream vouches to nourish and hydrate the skin. Deepika Padukone has been an ambassador of this product.
20. ***Himalaya fairness cream:*** The TVC claims that the cream, using natural ingredients like walnut, aloe vera, rose and orange, acts fast on tough skin of men. The advertisement also claims that the product is known to reduce pigmentation and show results within just four weeks of regular use.
21. ***Fairever cream:*** A product of 'CavinKare', the TVC for 'Fairever Fairness cream' offer consumers the unique and innovative 'Three Way Fairness Therapy' solution. The advertisement claims that the new 'Fairever' fairness cream scientifically extracts actives from nature to give a complete solution to all facial problems like skin darkening, blemishes; oiliness; dark circles & spots; and protection from sun, dirt and pollution.
22. ***Roop Amrit cream:*** The TVC of 'Roop Amrit Cream' claims to help its customers achieve the perfectly fair and spot-free skin that they have always dreamt of.
23. ***Meglow fairness cream***: The advertisement of the cream vouches of an upgraded formula with the latest brightening and whitening technology to target uneven skin tone, dark spots, fine lines and pigmentation. The product, through the commercial, assures of instant radiance and luminosity for the perfect look and feel.
24. ***Lakme Perfect Radiance Intense Whitening Day Creme***: The TVC has a voice over, 'Leave home with salon like fairness and turn the world into a ramp'. The advertisement claims that the product gives salon like fairness at home; and has skin polishing and de-tanning qualities.

Advertising related Laws in India

The Government of India has not set up a regulatory body in India to regulate advertisements. But as in due course depending on the nature of the grievances, the power to regulate advertisements may be exercised by a vast variety of authorities, including the courts, Central and state governments, tribunals or the police authorities. In addition to that, numerous legislations also deal with advertisement provisions in part, unfortunately, though not in total. (Refer Annexure - IV for the list of laws, rules and regulations that deal with advertisements.)

But, in cases related to colour discrimination, the following law/code count:

1. ***Constitution of India*:** Article 15 of The Constitution of India states:

15. Prohibition of discrimination on grounds of religion, race, caste, sex or place of birth

(1) The State shall not discriminate against any citizen on grounds only of religion, race, caste, sex, place of birth or any of them

(2) No citizen shall, on grounds only of religion, race, caste, sex, place of birth or any of them, be subject to any disability, liability, restriction or condition with regard to

  (a) access to shops, public restaurants, hotels and places of public entertainment; or

  (b) the use of wells, tanks, bathing ghats, roads and places of public resort maintained wholly or partly out of state funds or dedicated to the use of the general public

(3) Nothing in this article shall prevent the state from making any special provision for women and children

(4) Nothing in this article or in clause (2) of Article 29 shall prevent the State from making any special provision for the advancement of any socially and educationally backward classes of citizens or for the Scheduled Castes and the Scheduled Tribes.

2. ***The ASCI Code*:** To scrutinize certain principles and fairness in the sphere of advertising, 'Advertising Standards Council of India' was established in India in 1985. ASCI deals with complaints received from consumers and industry against such advertisements which are false, misleading, indecent, illegal, leading to unsafe practices or unfair to competition and are in contravention to the advertising code. Even though there is no such provision for regulating advertisement policy in the Constitution of India, which should be adopted by press or media, the Supreme Court has given guidelines for the same through a series of decisions.

3. ***Consumer Protection Act, 1986*:** Anyone can file such complaints with Consumer Forum for 'unfair trade practices' under section 2(1) (r) of

The Consumer Protection Act, 1986 which includes false claims made for a particular good.

The Act applies to all goods and services unless specifically exempted by the Central Government. It covers all the sectors whether private or public and any person. The provisions of the Act are compensatory as well as preventive and punitive in nature. The Act confers various rights on the consumers and envisages establishment of Consumer Protection Councils at the central, state, and district levels, the main objectives being: to promote and protect the rights of consumers; to provide a simple, speedy and inexpensive redressal of consumer grievances.

The Act envisages a three-tier quasi-judicial machinery at the national, state, and district levels. These are:

- National Consumer Disputes Redressal Commission known as National Commission,
- State Consumer Disputes Redressal Commissions known as State Commissions, and
- District Consumer Disputes Redressal Forum known as District Forum.

There are many ways by which consumers are exploited. A few of them are:

a. Selling at higher prices -- The price charged for the product will not be proportionate to the quality;
b. Product risk -- Drugs that are hazardous, banned or beyond expiry date; electrical appliances with inadequate safety precautions, etc;
c. Adulteration -- This is very common in food items and could prove to be highly injurious to one's health;
d. Sub-standard Products -- Items whose quality is far below the required standard;
e. False claims -- Manufacturers make false representations about their products in the media with a view to mislead the consumers. Claiming that use of a particular oil will cure baldness, using a company's fairness cream for a specific period will make one fair, etc., are all typical examples of exaggerated, misleading advertisements; and
f. Warranty/Annual Maintenance Contract -- In many cases, though the product will have a warranty or will be under Annual Maintenance Contract (AMC), when a problem arises, the consumer is told that certain parts will not be covered and they will have to pay.

The Consumer Protection Act, 1986, is definitely a blessing for consumers wronged by manufacturers or dealers.

4. ***The Drugs and Cosmetics Act, 1940*:** This law regulates the production, manufacture and sale of all drugs and cosmetics in the country. The Act prescribes a fine of up to Rs. 500 for any person using any report or extract of report of a test or analysis made by the Central Drugs Laboratory or a government analyst for advertising of a drug or cosmetic.

Cosmetics are governed by the Drugs and Cosmetics Act, 1940. The Act has been amended from time to time, with a view to maintain quality control. However, despite all these amendments, cosmetics manufacturers continue to use substandard raw material. What is more, there is virtually no check over the chemicals used in these cosmetics.

5. ***Indecent Representation of Women (Prohibition) Act, 1986*:** The Indecent Representation of Women (Prohibition) Act, 1986 forbids the depiction of women in an indecent or derogatory manner in the mass media. No person shall publish, or cause to be published, or arrange or take part in the publication or exhibition of, any advertisement which contains indecent representation of women in any form.
6. ***Cable Television Networks (Regulation) Act*:** Under the 'Cable Television Networks (Regulation) Act', the ministry issues directions to television channels or cable TV operators to stop airing an ad and not to the advertisers.

Role of ASCI:

Long regarded as a well intentioned but powerless body, the ASCI has revitalised itself over the last couple of years, moving with speed and aggression against advertisements that break its code of conduct.

In a memo issued in August 2014, ASCI outlined four guidelines for advertisers:

1. *Advertising should not communicate any discrimination as a result of skin colour. These advertisements should not reinforce negative social stereotyping on the basis of skin colour. Specifically, advertising should not directly or implicitly show people with darker skin, in a way which is widely seen as, unattractive, unhappy, depressed or concerned. These advertisements should not portray people with darker skin, in a way which is widely seen as, at a disadvantage of any kind, or inferior, or unsuccessful in any aspect of life particularly in relation to being attractive to the opposite sex, matrimony, job placement, promotions and other prospects.*

2. *In the pre-usage depiction of product, special care should be taken to ensure that the expression of the model/s in the real and graphical representation should not be negative in a way which is widely seen as unattractive, unhappy, depressed or concerned.*
3. *Advertising should not associate darker or lighter colour skin with any particular socio-economic strata, caste, community, religion, profession or ethnicity.*
4. *Advertising should not perpetuate gender based discrimination because of skin colour*

The guidelines from the 'Advertising Standards Council of India' (a self-regulatory body) that specifically targets several well-established tropes of fairness advertising ads, quite literally changed the face of advertising. In the approximately Rs 3,000-crore fairness category which includes creams, face washes and lotions, 'Hindustan Unilever' dominates the category with its 'Fair & Lovely' brand, and other big brands include 'Emami's Fair & Handsome' for men, as well as 'Garnier' from 'L'Oreal'.

The new rules propose, among other things, that advertising should not:

a. communicate any discrimination as a result of skin colour,
b. directly or implicitly show people with darker skin as unattractive, unhappy, depressed or concerned,
c. portray people with darker skin as at a disadvantage of any kind, or inferior, or unsuccessful in any aspect of life particularly in relation to being attractive to the opposite sex, matrimony, job placement, promotions and other prospects,
d. use post production visual effects on the model/s to show exaggerated product efficacy or associate darker or lighter colour skin with any particular socio-economic strata, caste, community, religion, profession or ethnicity,
e. perpetuate gender-based discrimination based on skin colour.

According to Sam Balsara, chairman and managing director, Madison World and a former chairman of ASCI, the reason for these guidelines is to make it clear to advertisers as to what the society finds acceptable and what it doesn't.[7]

When asked about the ramifications on the guidelines on its advertising, a spokes-person from Hindustan Unilever, said, that the ASCI's move to further and strengthen guidelines, is welcomed; as this will help in promoting transparency in advertising.[8]

A spokesperson from Garnier, added that they strongly believe advertising should not encourage social discrimination of people based on aspects like the colour of their skin; and thus, 'Garnier' always focuses on the efficacy of the product in almost all their communication ,which is backed by scientific fact.[8]

Shweta Purandare, secretary general at the ASCI, says that the organisation receives several complaints, over the years, against advertisements regarding skin lightening or fairness improvement.[8]

Partha Rakshit, chairman, ASCI, said that the new guidelines would help advertisers comply with ASCI code's Chapter III 1 b, which states that advertisements should not deride any race, caste, colour, creed or nationality.[9]

Former ASCI chairman and consultative committee member Bharat Patel said that the feedback to the draft guidelines was positive. "Advertisers have reconciled to the fact that they cannot show dark-skinned people as depressed or disadvantaged in any manner. Fairness brands cannot deride any skin colour," he said.[10]

TV advertisements will have to comply with the guidelines, as the 'Cable Television Networks (Regulation) Act' makes it mandatory for all television commercials to abide by ASCI rules.

Srinivasan Swamy, ASCI board member told '*The Hindu*', "Fairness is a large product market of about Rs. 4,000 crore and advertising from it is about Rs. 600 crore."[10]

Responding to the new guidelines issued by ASCI, Mohan Goenka, Director, Emami Ltd, said, "We welcome the new advertising guidelines of ASCI for the skin whitening products category which address the concerns raised by various quarters including industry, society and consumers at large. The aim of an advertiser should be to ensure that viewers are not misguided about the efficacy of any product or promote discrimination of any sort, without compromising the creative licence to portray product attributes. We believe that consumer is the king...and it should finally be his choice to use any product that is advertised."[11]

Darshan Patel, Chairman and Managing Director of Vini Cosmetics Pvt. Ltd that markets 'White Tone' said that although the product does not promise 'fairness', his firm will abide by the ASCI rules.[10]' 'White Tone' talks of looking good as it is a make-up powder and 'Glam-up', a foundation cream from the same parent company, vouches of looking special.

Celebrities Advocating Fairness Creams

In an India, where the educated classes are increasingly demanding a social conscience and accountability from their stars, celebrities these days face an interesting dilemma when they agree to be the face of a fairness product. After all, it's not easy trying to position yourself as a sensitive and liberal star, when the product you endorse cashes in on the widely prevalent prejudice against dark skin in our country.

Genelia D'Souza (Garnier), John Abraham (Garnier's fairness moisturiser for men), Priyanka Chopra (Pond's White Beauty), Sonam Kapoor (L'Oreal's Pearl Perfect) and Shah Rukh Khan (Fair & Handsome), Deepika Padukone (Johnson & Johnson's Neutrogena skincare range that includes its Neutrogena Fine Fairness cream), Shahid Kapoor (Vaseline's whitening cream) among many others, have endorsed skin whitening products.

Celebrities Denouncing Fairness Creams

In our country, where standards of political correctness are changing, clearly these stars are torn between the large sections of their fan followings, who use fairness creams; and another section that accuses them of being racist, colour prejudiced and socially irresponsible when they endorse these products.

Today's advertisements try to be more positive and understated. 'Glow', 'radiance' and 'brightness' have become catchphrases in commercials featuring major celebrities for products that promise an even skin tone and a removal of blemishes, but quietly tucked away in a corner somewhere the word 'fairness' will peep out.

1. Ranbir Kapoor: He rejected an offer from a major manufacturer simply because he doesn't believe in what the product stands for. He believes that it is a big responsibility and not just a money thing. He has to be careful, believe in it; and be honest to what he is endorsing.
2. Bipasha Basu: Bipasha has always refused the offers to endorse skin whitening products. She believes that we are all beautiful the way nature made us and we should accept ourselves that way.
4. Kangana Ranaut: Kangana Ranaut has also refused to endorse fairness creams. Her reason is that it would be insulting her sister who 'is dusky, yet beautiful'.
5. Nandita Das: Actor Nandita Das has lent her star power to the 'Dark is Beautiful' campaign, which was launched in 2009. She revealed that, as a child, she often got comments like "Poor thing, she is so dark". She turned down the request of the directors who wanted her to use make-up to look fairer.

The Debate

A L'Oreal India spokesperson says, "The communication for L'Oreal India's fairness products focuses on their efficacy and is done in a manner that is ethical, responsible and backed by scientific fact. We do not play up the social discrimination and insecurities of people in the communication for any of our brands." "In a culture where mothers-to-be take huge amounts of dairy products in the hope of having a fair baby, I would say the obsession with fair skin is already deep-rooted," said Ms Zenobia Pithawalla, Executive creative director of 'Ogilvy & Mather India'.[12]

Dr Anuj Pall, consultant dermatologist at Max Hospital, Gurgaon says, "These over-the-counter products only even out skin tone if the person has normal skin, so maybe the user feels that they've become fairer but they've not. Even their claims of removing a tan and acne marks is questionable, since those acne marks and temporary tan will go away anyway, if left to themselves."[13] But there is a more dangerous aspect to these so-called fairness products that goes beyond political correctness. Dr Shehla Aggarwal, skin specialist and Director, Mehak Skin Clinic, Delhi, says that the Indian skin produces a dark melanin that acts as a protection when exposed to the sun. The melanin also has the property to prevent cancer, and it is this element that makes our skin age less. These fairness products bleach the melanin. So a long-term use of fairness products could cause ageing and perhaps even skin cancer. The Indian dermatologists' community doesn't want to cause a cancer scare but it's been about 30 years since 'Fair & Lovely' was launched in the Indian market and the impact is likely to be felt in the coming years.[13]

With so much controversy on these products, it is clear that the brands need to offer incredible amount of money to celebrities to bring them on board. Shah Rukh Khan remains the highest paid of the lot, John Abraham gets anywhere from Rs 2-3.5 crore a year for a product endorsement, Priyanka Chopra and Deepika Padukone are paid in the range of Rs 2-3 crore per annum, Shahid Kapoor earns Rs 2-2.5 crore, Sonam Kapoor gets Rs 1.5-2 crore and the figure for Genelia is Rs 1.5 crore.[13]

Celebrities have another incredible benefit too. These advertisements translate into high visibility for them as brand ambassadors.

Shruti Swetambhari, CEO of celebrity and brand management firm 'Green Leaf Sports and Entertainment', tries to bring a balance to the debate by explaining that the advertisements recently have become more refined. "When brands like 'Garnier' and 'L'Oreal' entered the market, fairness products immediately shot into an A-list category of products that became desirable and acceptable to big stars; and the stars are also more comfortable with the fact that these advertisements no longer talk about a dark person becoming white, but about healthy skin."[13]

Suggestions

1. It is an undisputed fact that advertisement plays a vital role in building up any business. The aim of advertisement is to attract the customers and enhance the visibility of the products and services of the company among the consumers. Advertisements help a company build its brand image in the minds of the viewers. Therefore, nowadays, companies spend a huge amount of their resources on advertising and promotional strategies. Thus, it is evident that there are no specific legislations governing advertising in India, other than ASCI; which itself is in need for more teeth. It is evident that the need of the hour is a codified uniform legislation for advertising related issues.
2. We should have such laws that are binding on both the producers and advertisers of the products. Unless the laws are strict, advertisers will not be cautious regarding their violations of other's rights.
3. It is also the duty of the aware citizens and institutions like judiciary to raise their voice through Public Interest Litigations against airing of such advertisements on national television.
4. Under the 'Cable Television Networks (Regulation) Act', the Ministry issues directions to television channels or cable TV operators to stop airing an advertisement and not to the advertisers. But, unless the advertisers are booked and given penalty, the menace of such offensive advertisements would be seen more often in national television.
5. The government must announce very strict penalties for shopkeepers, beauty parlours and vendors of cosmetics who sell or use products which are fake, labelled or do not carry even the minimum required statutory information under the packaged 'Commodities Act' (such as the name of the manufacturer, to whom the liability can be attributed). If a producer of fake and spurious products is deprived of a sales outlet, he will go out of business. In the case of imported cosmetics, the name and address of the importer must be clearly mentioned and it should be made clear by law that the importer will be legally responsible if the safety aspect of the product is ignored or overlooked.
6. The Government should publish a list of known toxic chemicals that are banned for use in cosmetics and toiletries. This should be made known

to the industry, associations, and through them, to their constituents. Any deliberate use of banned chemicals should be severely penalized. Stringent action should be taken against the owners/directors as well as the senior officials of the manufacturing units deliberately using banned substances or manufacturing fake or spurious cosmetics.

7. Manufacture of cosmetics and toiletries should not be permitted without a valid manufacturing license. Records of each manufacturer must be maintained by the state government, which should renew licences only if there are no serious cases pending against the manufacturer. The licence number must be made part of the labelling requirements.
8. The government should seriously investigate whether some form of certifying label can be awarded to those products that do not contain harmful substances.
9. The standards for cosmetics and toiletries should be universally applicable, irrespective of whether or not a product contains 'herbal' ingredients. Back-passing between different departments of the government should not be allowed. An educational campaign, demonstrating that so-called 'herbal' or 'Ayurvedic' cosmetics that can also be very harmful, should be launched, so that consumers are not lulled into a false sense of security.
10. And finally, the government, reputed manufacturers and consumer groups should join hands to inform the consumer of what is safe and what is not.

Exception of 'Tanishq' Advertisement

Jewellery retailer 'Tanishq' has come up with a commercial that moves away from the stereotype of blushing, fair-skinned brides and introduces the concept of remarriage—possibly for the first time in Indian advertising. The advertisement, shot by filmmaker Gauri Shinde of *English Vinglish* movie fame, showcases a dusky bride—theatre actor Priyanka Bose, looking at herself in the mirror as she gets ready for the wedding. A little girl runs up to her and chatters away. They walk towards the *mandap* together. The little girl settles down between her grandparents to watch the wedding unfold, but soon wants to participate in the *pheras* with the bride and groom. On being shushed into silence, the little girl sits back disappointed. On seeing this, the groom calls out to the girl and carries her through the *pheras*. The commercial ends with the little girl asking the groom if she can call him 'Daddy'.

The TVC, created by 'Lowe Lintas India', has received much praise.

In a society where there is still some premium placed on light skin, this new advertisement by 'Tanishq' was seen as defying accepted stereotypes surrounding the depiction of beauty in the mainstream media.

In an interview with 'India Today', director Gauri Shinde (who went on to win many awards for her debut feature film *English Vinglish*), stated that the use of a 'dusky' model was not deliberate. She said, "I don't see these differences between dusky and fair and frankly I personally don't even want to be part of that debate because I feel there is a complex at play; against the dusky, against the fair. It's unnecessary. Everyone's beautiful."[13] 'Tanishq' has not only defied the unethical standards prevalent in the world of Indian advertisement, but also for taking on socially relevant issues in India.

Conclusion

Launching his line of skin bleaching products in 2011, Jamaican artist Vybz Kartel, said that when black women would stop straightening their hair and wearing wigs, and when white women would stop getting implants; then he would stop using the 'cake soap' and all would live naturally ever after. However in June 2013, he appeared to have changed his views, and was seen encouraging youngsters to stop bleaching.[14]

It is to be reiterated that, according to revenue data, colourism is neither reserved for African-Americans nor are they the largest consumers of such products. Japan comes first, with China and India contributing to 13 per cent growth each year. By 2018, the skin-whitening industry is projected to evolve globally into a $20 billion business.[15]

However, large scale consumers of such products span Tokyo, India, Shanghai, Lagos, Kuala Lumpar, Manila, New York and London. Yet, the industry is increasingly catching the ire of public and authorities; and is being presented with major corporate social responsibility and business ethics issues.[15]

In July 2013, a Japanese company 'Kanebo' had to recall a skin lightening product as approximately fifteen thousand consumers suffered from skin reaction. They were left with white patches as large as 2-inches in diameter. It was a side effect of the agent Rhododenol, which is used to brighten skin. The company is now faced with paying medical costs of their customers. [15]

Later in Thailand, the corporate practices of 'Unilever' and 'Vogue' have been brought into question. Unilever broadcast a TVC, directly correlating the fairness of one's skin to their level of education, which got pulled out.

Similarly, published an image of Naomi Campbell on its cover; wherein she appeared a shade fairer. The artist in question, in his defence, claimed that he always uses pastels in his photographic artwork, as officially stated by Vogue's CEO.[15]

However, in India, the television advertisers have been only debating on the lines of demand and supply rather than accepting the unethical character of these advertisements. A few changes should be made at the ground-level to deal with the concept of colourism that is so deeply ingrained in the minds of most Indian citizens. Some of these changes are mentioned as follows:

First, to challenge the validity of colourism.

Second, to raise awareness, to educate people globally about the history of colourism and the negative impacts it has had on the health and wellbeing on individuals and societies.

Third, to encourage responsible business practices and consumerism.

Fourth, to lobby for greater regulation and removal of products which are not only harmful to people and the environment, but which also reinforce racist attitudes and social stratifications based on skin colour.

If we all become responsible and work together for the protection against discrimination on the basis of skin colour, then our society would feel more secured and protected.

References

1 *Colorism - definition and synonims of «colorism» in English dictionary.* (n.d.). Retrieved from http://englishdictionary.education/en/colorism

2 Schultz, E. A., & Lavenda, R. H. (2005). *Cultural Anthropology: A perspective on the human condition.* New York: Oxford University Press.

3 *Constitution of The People's Republic Of Bangladesh.* (n.d.). Retrieved from http://hrlibrary.umn.edu/research/bangladesh-constitution.pdf

4 Journey of fairness creams' advertising in India - Page2 - *The Economic Times.* (n.d.). Retrieved from http://economictimes.indiatimes.com/features/brand-equity/journey-of-fairness-creams-advertising-in-india/articleshow/msid-30997189,curpg-2.cms?from=mdr

5 *Don't show bias on basis of skin colour: ASCI to fairness cream brands like HUL, Emami | MxM India.* (n.d.). Retrieved from http://www.mxmindia.com/2014/06/dont-show-bias-on-basis-of-skin-colour-asci-to-fairness-cream-brands-like-hul-emami/

6 *The crazy skin-lightening ads that have been banned in India - Digiday.* (n.d.). Retrieved from http://digiday.com/brands/four-ads-wont-see-indian-television-ever/

7 *Don't show bias on basis of skin colour: ASCI to fairness cream brands like HUL, Emami | MxM India.* (n.d.). Retrieved from http://www.mxmindia.com/2014/06/dont-show-bias-on-basis-of-skin-colour-asci-to-fairness-cream-brands-like-hul-emami/

8 Balakrishnan, R., & Bhatt, S. (2014, June 11). *Change in the Air in Ad World - Fairness Norms Now in Black and White - Mumbai -The Economic Times.* Retrieved from http://epaperbeta.timesofindia.com/Article.aspx?eid=31818&articlexml=CHANGE-IN-THE-AIR-IN-AD-WORLD-Fairness-11062014001083

9 *ASCI to rein in ads featuring skin lightening products* - The Hindu. (n.d.). Retrieved from http://www.thehindu.com/business/Industry/asci-to-rein-in-ads-featuring-skin-lightening-products/article6104818.ece

10 *Guidelines to ensure 'fair' play in advertising* - National - *The Hindu.* (n.d.). Retrieved from http://www.thehindu.com/todays-paper/tp-national/guidelines-to-ensure-fair-play-in-advertising/article6105981.ece

11 annavetticadgoes2themovies: Stars Who Endorse Fairness Products / Article Pulished in *The New Indian Express.* (n.d.). Retrieved from http://annavetticadgoes2themovies.blogspot.in/2015/04/stars-who-endorse-fairness-products.html

12 *Vanity fair- The New Indian Express.* (n.d.). Retrieved from http://www.newindianexpress.com/magazine/2011/jun/26/vanity-fair-266689.html

13 Gauri Shinde, the woman behind the Tanishq remarriage ad : India, News - *India Today.* (n.d.). Retrieved from http://indiatoday.intoday.in/story/tanishq-reamarriage-ad-gauri-shinde/1/320656.html

14 *Challenging the Ethics of Colorism: The Future Is Bright.* (n.d.). Retrieved from http://www.csrwire.com/blog/posts/1099-challenging-the-ethics-of-colourism-the-future-is-bright

15 'Portrayal of colour discrimination vis-à-vis Indian television advertisements' in the *International Journal* of the International Organization of Scientific Research Journal of Humanities and Social Science (IOSR-JHSS) *Volume 20, Issue 5*, Ver. VI (May. 2015), PP 45-64 e-ISSN: 2279-0837, p-ISSN: 2279-0845.

7

Peace and Communal Harmony

Advertising Vis-a-vis Human Rights

India is known as the land of unity in diversity; and of all seasons and contrast. It is appropriately called the 'culminating point' or the 'melting point' of all human cultures, religions and races. No country can be constituted of perfectly homogenous people. Every country, therefore, has to confront the problem of minorities and national integration. Social, cultural, ethnic, political, economic and historical antagonisms are bound to arise in a country of mixed character. There is no sovereign remedy to eliminate the majority-minority problem; which in our case is mainly between the Hindu and Muslim communities.

Concept of 'Communal Harmony' through Television Advertisements

'Kaun Banega Crorepati' promo of the year 2014 was bitter-sweet portrayal on the sad existence of Hindu-Muslim divide in our country.[1,2]

Brooke Bond Red Label, with its brand proposition – 'Swad Apnepan Ka' or the 'Taste of Togetherness', has always tried to brew togetherness among families and diverse communities; the idea being that tea melts away differences.[3] Its 2014 advertisement garnered quite an appraisal when it portrayed a reluctant Hindu family bonding with their Muslim neighbour, over a few cups of Red Label tea. The TVC was both appreciated for its subtle effort in trying to bridge the invisible; yet perpetuating religious divide in the country as well as criticised for portraying Hindus as intolerant or unwelcoming towards Muslims.

Havells HiMu TVC of 2013, from one of its 'Hava badlegi campaign', came out with an interesting social message that reiterates our Constitution's provision for religious freedom.

Holcim subsidiary 'Ambuja cement' has always pitched the strength of its product using the 'unbreakable wall' as a central theme. The Ambuja Cement TVC promotes that the walls that create divisions between communities should be broken down.

Case Studies

Four case studies which became a huge sensation on national television very recently in India are discussed.

1. Havells Fan: HiMu 'hawa badlegi'
2. KBC: cutting across the divide
3. Brooke Bond Red Label: brewing togetherness
4. Ambuja Cement: 'Classroom TVC'

Havells Fan

The TVC, released in 2013, shows a couple getting discharged from a hospital after delivering a baby girl. When the nurse asked the father the reason of his mentioning the religion of the child as 'HiMu', the latter explains that it is the combination of 'Hindu' and 'Muslim' and that their daughter can adopt any religion she likes when she grows up.

Going beyond product features, the TVC introduces and encourages a change in mind-sets. The campaign, conceptualised by Lowe Lintas, comprises four films of which 'HiMu' deals with promotion of communal harmony. The TVC has been directed by Anupam Mishra of Crazy Few Films.

Amer Jaleel, national creative director, Lowe Lintas & Partners, explains that that instead of an attempt to change the mindset of people, the campaign merely chronicles the change; thereby thinking that the best way to get into people's mind in such a low-involvement category like fan was to put the brand in your head.[4]

Vedobroto Roy, executive creative director, Dentsu Communications, says that the campaign, with its wow factor, will leave its mark as the rationale leaves a lot to the imagination - that is what makes Havells fans different from the rest.[4]

Divyapratap Mehta, chief strategy officer, Publicis Capital says that even though the TVC has caught the attention of the audience with a very powerful societal insight; they would not know why they should buy the product and what exactly the brand stands for. However, the TVC has no connection with the category or the brand.[4]

Kaun Banega Crorepati

The second promo-film of the eighth edition of 'Kaun Banega Crorepati' campaign dwells on the Hindu-Muslim divide in our country; the first promo being based on discrimination against the people of 'The Northeast India'. The TVC, released in 2014, portrays a Hindu boy trying to bridge the religious differences with a Muslim family that stays in the same locality; thereby moving beyond 'individuals' to talk about 'unity of the people'.

While the broader thought behind the campaign remains the same – 'Yahan Sirf Paise Nahi, Dil Bhi Jeete Jate Hain' (money is just not won here, but hearts too), the TVC brings out the communal issues between Hindus and Muslims.

The advertisement portrays a small neighbourhood where a Hindu and a Muslim family live. The son in the Hindu family, Ankit, has been selected for 'Kaun Banega Crorepati' and is about to step of the main gate when one of the sons in the Muslim family sneezes. Sneezing before some auspicious occasion is considered to be a bad omen by Hindus but Ankit's father stops his other son from retaliating.

On the hot seat, when confronted with a tough question, Ankit opts for a 'phone a friend' lifeline. The show is being viewed live by both the families. He calls the head of the Muslim family and asks him the meaning of 'Assalam-walekum'. The old man's hatred evaporates as he turns emotional and answers the question saying "Khuda Tumhe Salamaat Rakhe" (May peace be upon you). As Ankit wins, both the heads of the families come out and hug each other.

The Hindu-Muslim TVC also showcases the fact that the new generation does not believe in the divide and can unite people of these two religions.

KBC's campaigns have, over the years, been about knowledge – 'Sirf Gyaan Hi Aapko Aapka Haq Dilata Hai' (only knowledge can give you your rights), 'Ek sawaal jo aapki zindagi badal de' (a question that changes your life), 'Koi bhi insaan chhota nahi hota' (no person is insignificant) and 'Seekhna band, toh jeetna band' (stop learning, stop winning).

Gaurav Seth, Marketing head, SET says that the show, along with its host Mr. Amitabh Bachchan, will showcase social transformation by portraying stories of everyday heroes and community bonding; thereby, igniting hope and positivity in the hearts of the nation.[5,6]

Saurabh Varma, CEO, Leo Burnett India, added that 'Kaun Banega Crorepati' advertisements use the power of communication effectively to raise the collective conscience of the nation. The participants that make it to the hot seat take more than just money from the KBC stage; and the latest promos take this insight to a larger, national and social canvas.[7]

Vikram Pandey, Executive director, Leo Burnett India feels that 'Kaun Banega Crorepati' provides for an opportunity to affect many more people.

Jitender Dabas, EVP and head of planning, McCann Erickson is of the view that some might find the execution a bit melodramatic but the Bollywood-style treatment will only make it foolproof for the mass audience which 'Kaun Banega Crorepati' is trying to reach; thereby the themes like regional or communal harmony shall always make for a winning emotional and moral appeal.[6]

Contrary to the above views K S Chakravarthy (Chax), NCD, FCBUlka, expressing his misgivings on this particular leg of what has been one of his favourite campaigns over the years, says that he believes that the advertisement does not have a compelling story, is built on the same shaky premise, the detailing weakens the telling at every level, the script is pretty unimaginative, the casting is distinctly clichéd and the handling of the characters and emotions is uniformly unconvincing.[6]

Brooke Bond Red Label

In its 2014 campaign, Brooke Bond Red Label moved beyond the idea of connecting families and positioned 'tea' as a beverage that binds diverse communities. Ogilvy India is the agency behind the campaign. The film is executed by Purple Vishnu Films and directed by Sainath Choudhury.

In its latest TVC, Brooke Bond Red Label positions both—the brand and the product—as the first brick to bridge between communities. The minute long commercial dwells on the sensitive theme - the Hindu-Muslim divide in India.

The campaign shows a visibly Hindu couple locked outside their own house. As the wife is seen searching for the keys in her purse, their neighbour, a burkha-clad woman invites them over for tea as they must be tired. She requests them to wait at her place till they find their keys. The husband, shown uncomfortable with her religion, turns down the offer. His wife tries to coax him saying that the fragrance of tea is very good from the neighbour's house (*Chai ki bahut achchi khushboo aati hai iske ghar se* means Her house emits aroma of good tea). While her words fail to convince him, the aroma of fresh tea does the trick. The couple ends up enjoying a cup of tea with their neighbour; with the husband asking for another cup. The catchphrase used at the end of the ad is 'Swad Apnepan Ka' (taste of affinity).

Abhijit Avasthi, National creative director, Ogilvy India says that this particular TVC was about bringing together people across communities unlike previous campaigns that talked about bringing family members together; and that the Hindu-Muslim plot is one that most audiences can relate to and as the intention of the brand is to strike an emotional chord with the consumers. The TVC, in a creative and compelling manner, aims to highlight the fact that people bond with each other over tea.

Even though Anupama Ramaswamy, Group creative director, Cheil India, applauds the effort and the creative execution, she feels that the religious angle is something the commercial could do without further insisting that, given the way we live our lives today, often, we don't even know our neighbours.[6]

Raghu Bhat, Founder director, Scarecrow Communications, felt that the TVC was timely given the 2014 election campaigns that were 'dividing people.' The best thing about the film, according to him, is the fact that "it uses story-telling to spread this message instead of preaching," a trick that was bound to yield a higher level of acceptance. He believes that the product's 'unique selling points' of 'khushbu' (aroma) and 'swad' (taste) is at the heart of the campaign; making it a commendable piece of communication.

Ambuja Cement: 'Classroom TVC'

Released in 2014 the TVC was created by Publicis South Asia, a creative agency that is part of the Publicis Omnicom Group.[7]

Set in a school classroom, the film featured a teacher asking one of the students, Arjun who was disturbing students around him, to read his essay on the subject 'Wall'. He starts saying that there are two kinds of walls – good walls and bad walls; and all the students in the classroom burst out in laughter. When she asks him to elaborate without beating around the bush, he hesitatingly spells out the core message of the commercial. And this is where the tone of the film changes. He speaks of his friend Iqbal, who is very good at cricket, but has stopped playing with them of late. He says that his uncle has alerted him about a wall that stands between them - a wall that he cannot see. A voice over kicks in as the students and teacher listen spellbound: 'We must break down those walls which give rise to disharmony and disparity between people; and for strong walls, only Ambuja Cement.'

In less words, the campaign touched upon the issue of communal divide between people; a sensitive advertisement that is especially relevant in the Indian context.

Ajay Kapur, deputy MD and CEO, Ambuja Cement, noted that strength being a key aspect of the product, the commercial merges with the brand proposition. [8]

Partha Sinha, director, South Asia, Publicis, and the agency's chief strategy officer, believes that the TVC will take the element of 'strength' associated with the brand to the next level.[8]

Vivek Deshpande, head, brands and marketing strategies, Ambuja Cement, says the idea was to shift from the concept of strength from a mere physical entity to a more exalted one.[8]

Advertising related Laws in India

The Government of India has not set up a regulatory body in India to regulate advertisements. But as in due course depending on the nature of the grievances, the power to regulate advertisements may be exercised by a vast variety of authorities, including the courts, Central and state governments, tribunals or the police authorities. In addition to that, numerous legislations also deal with advertisement provisions in part, unfortunately, though not in total. (Refer Annexure - IV for the list of laws, rules and regulations that deal with advertisements.)

But only the following talk of promotion of religious harmony:

1. ***The Constitution of India***: The Constitution of India does not provide for a state religion.

Article 19 gives all citizens the right to freedom of speech and expression but subject to "reasonable restrictions" for preserving inter alia "public order, decency or morality".

Article 25(1) states, "Subject to public order, morality and health and to the other provisions of this Part, all persons are equally entitled to freedom of conscience and the right freely to profess, practise and propagate religion".

Article 28 prohibits any religious instruction in any educational institution wholly maintained out of state funds.

Article 51A(h) imposes on every citizen the duty to develop the scientific temper, humanism and the spirit of inquiry and reform.

2. ***Indian Penal Code, 1860***:
   a. *Section 153A* of the penal code says, inter alia:Whoever (a) by words, either spoken or written, or by signs or by visible representations or otherwise, promotes or attempts to promote, on grounds of religion, race, place of birth, residence, language, caste or community or any other ground whatsoever, disharmony or feelings of enmity, hatred or ill-will between different religious, racial, language or regional groups or castes or communities, or (b) commits any act which is prejudicial to the maintenance of harmony between

different religious, racial, language or regional groups or castes or communities, and which disturbs or is likely to disturb the public tranquillity, . . . shall be punished with imprisonment which may extend to three years, or with fine, or with both.

b. *Section 295(A)* of the Indian Penal Code (IPC) says: Whoever, with deliberate and malicious intention of outraging the religious feelings of any class of (citizens of India), (by words, either spoken or written, or by signs or by visible representations or otherwise), insults or attempts to insult the religion or the religious beliefs of that class, shall be punished with imprisonment of either description for a term which may extend to (three years), or with fine, or with both.[11]

3. ***Government Initiatives*:** The government has set up the Ministry of Minority Affairs, the National Human Rights Commission (NHRC) and the National Commission for Minorities (NCM) to investigate religious discrimination and to make recommendations for redressal to the local authorities. Though they do not have any power, local and central authorities generally follow them. These organisations have investigated numerous instances of religious tension including the implementation of "anti-conversion" bills in numerous states, the 2002 Gujarat violence and the 2008 attacks against Christians in Orissa.
4. ***Advertising Standards Council of India (ASCI):*** Standards of conduct – Clause III states that no advertisement shall be permitted which: Tends to incite people to crime or to promote disorder and violence or intolerance, derides any race, caste, colour, creed or nationality, presents criminality as desirable or directly or indirectly encourages people - particularly minors - to emulate it or conveys the modus operandi of any crime or adversely affects friendly relations with a foreign State.
5. ***Press Council of India – Norms of journalistic conduct*:** The following are the several areas wherein the aspect of communal harmony has been highlighted:

   a. *Right to privacy*: Things concerning a person's home, family, religion, health, sexuality, personal life and private affairs are covered by the concept of privacy excepting where any of these infringes upon the public or public interest.

   b. *Caste, religion or community references*:

      i. An accused or a victim shall not be described by his caste or community when the same does not have anything to do with the offence or the crime and plays no part either in the identification of any accused or proceeding, if there be any.

- ii Newspaper should not publish any fictional literature distorting and portraying the religious or well known characters in an adverse light offending the susceptibilities of large sections of society who hold those characters in high esteem, invested with attributes of the virtuous and lofty.
- iii. Commercial exploitation of the name of prophets, seers or deities is repugnant to journalistic ethics and good taste.
- iv. It is the duty of the newspaper to ensure that the tone, spirit and language of a write up is not objectionable, provocative, against the unity and integrity of the country, spirit of the constitution, seditious and inflammatory in nature or designed to promote communal disharmony. It should also not attempt to promote balkanisation of the country.

c. *Norms for observance by the Press in the wake of communal disturbances 1969*: Making disrespectful, derogatory or insulting remarks on or reference to the different religions or faiths or their founders.

6. ***Doordarshan – Code for Commercial Advertising*:** General rules for conduct in advertising:
   1. Advertising shall be so designed as to conform to the laws of the country and shall not offend the morality, decency and the religious susceptibilities of the people.
7. ***Programme and Advertising Codes –The Cable Television Network Rules, 1994*:** Rule 6. Programme Code (1) No programme should be carried in the cable service which
   (a) Offends against good taste or decency;
   (b) Contains criticism of friendly countries;
   (c) Contains attack on religions or communities or visuals or words contemptuous of religious groups or which promote communal attitudes.

Suggestions

1. It is a fact that most advertisers do not like to bag controversial topics but making more ads on the lines of promoting communal harmony would go a long way in uniting the two religious communities – Hindus and Muslims.
2. 'Catch them young' is a very important phrase that advertisers should always keep in mind while making ads on communal harmony. Incorporating children of different communities in the ads and

showing them in happy and friendly light will have more impact on the viewers.

3. Fostering communal harmony should be an important agenda for advertisers at the present age where communal unrest has become a regular affair.

Conclusion

India, ever since time immemorial, has been successfully weaving diverse alien influences and giving them local colour; making the country a hub of cultural, linguistic and religious interaction. The traces have been so inextricably woven into the fabric of our society, that it is impossible to separate the strands of what was once alien from what is indigenous. This has made the Indian culture composite in nature.

National integration through communal harmony has always been an important objective of the Indian Government. In the current era, when India is marching ahead on the path of economic development and acquiring a glorious place on the world stage, the need of the hour is to preserve, promote and defend the secular, pluralistic, socialist and democratic values of our Constitution.

However, over the years, the problem of communalism has adversely affected the progress of the country. The government and other relevant agencies have made focussed efforts to contain the problem and promote harmony among the various communities of the nation. It has now been widely recognized that the media can play a very effective role in promoting communal harmony and national integration.

The onus is on the government and various other agencies including the media to help mould public opinion to foster friendly and harmonious relations between various communities and religious groups; thereby promoting peace and communal harmony along with national solidarity.

Media is one of the most potent and effective medium to maintain and strengthen communal harmony. The need for mobilizing peace and harmony at the national as well as grass root level, the need for creating an awareness of the dangers involved in communal hatred and conflicts and of the need for joining hands and protesting against such divisive and destructive forces is now strongly felt. The biggest challenge is to merge the religious, linguistic and regional identity into a national identity, while maintaining the other identities and cultures. Media has the potential to play a very important role in bringing over this change.

Television advertisements is one such area through which media can achieve their goals of promoting communal harmony and thereby promote national integration; and prove that it is true that portrayal of religious harmony in television ads is a positive step towards building Hindu-Muslim unity in India. But, the researcher believes that we are only assuming an ideal outcome. The facts and figures in daily news show that communal disharmony is on the rise. The Havells fan television advertisement was broadcast in 2013; the same year when there were hindu-muslim riots in West Bengal when a Muslim cleric was killed by unidentified assailants and in the Muzaffarnagar district of Uttar Pradesh where the two communities again spurted violence. Thus, the outcome of such television advertisements seem less impactful on the psyche of our religiously diverse citizens.

Moreover, the researcher also feels that most of the times the advertisers choose controversial topics to garner attention for their product. But, one small step from their end is good enough to bring about social change in due course of time.

References

1 Pathak, J. P. (2016). *Portrayal of communal harmony: An analysis of Indian TV Ads.* Retrieved from www.questjournals.org/jrhss/papers/vol4-issue7/F475057.pdf

2 *This Kaun Banega Crorepati Ad On Hindu-Muslim Harmony Will Blow Your Mind Away - Youth Connect.* (n.d.). Retrieved from http://www.youthconnect.in/2014/.../kaun-banega-crorepati-ad-on-hindu-muslim-harmony/

3 *After Hindu-Muslim Neighbor Ad, Red Label Tea Touches Upon Live-in Relationships In New Ad | Lighthouse Insights.* (n.d.). Retrieved from http://lighthouseinsights.in/red-label-tea-ive-in-relationships-ad-new-ad.html/

4 *Havells fans: For a change.* (n.d.). Retrieved from http://www.afaqs.com/news/story/36920_Havells-fans-For-a-change

5 *KBC: cutting across the divide.* (n.d.). Retrieved from http://www.afaqs.com/news/story/41437_KBC-cutting-across-the-divide

6 *Brewing Togetherness.* (n.d.). Retrieved from http://www.afaqs.com/news/story/40559_Brewing-Togetherness

7 *Breaking Down Walls of Disparity.* (n.d.). Retrieved from http://www.afaqs.com/news/story/40601_Breaking-Down-Walls-Of-Disparity

8 *Ambuja Cement builds awareness, urges India to break invisible walls of divisiveness | Advertising | Campaign India.* (n.d.). Retrieved from http://www.campaignindia.in/video/ambuja-cement-builds-awareness-urges-india-to-break-invisible-walls-of-divisiven/420647

8

Portrayal of Peace and Harmony between Nations

Advertising vis-a-vis Human Rights

There is no bias in highlighting the portrayal of India-Pakistan relationship only even though India has many other neighbouring countries too. Indian television advertisements have mostly highlighted the relationship between the two countries only; and there have been rare instances where the relationship between India and any other country has been portrayed. Thus, we have chosen what has been majorly portrayed by the Indian television channels; without any personal bias or prejudice of our own.

Case Studies

1. *8PM Whisky – The Generals*:

Enterprise Nexus Communications was the advertising agency for the product. It was released in Jan 1999. The successful TV commercial showed generals of two enemy countries (assumingly India and Pakistan) sharing a drink at the border. The voiceover says, "8PM – a time for friends."

This TVC was probably the first of the sorts; and, as such, not much details was available.[1]

2. *Airtel – Barriers Break When People Talk*:

In the TVC that was released in December 2007, Airtel shifted away from its usual 'Express Yourself' premise making the idea of breaking the communication barriers as its focal point; thereby making 'Barriers Break When People Talk' as its new mantra. Even though the commercial is hinted at the perpetual LoC conflicts between India and Pakistan, the idea can be extrapolated to much larger audience in general.[2]

The advertisement was conceptualised by Chax, Ajay Gahlaut, Abhinav Pratiman and Daniel Upputuru of Rediffusion DY&R. The commercial was shot by Prakash Varma of Nirvana Films in Morocco.[2]

The TVC begins on the shot of a boy eating at home, when he sees a football land on his balcony. He steps out to find another boy on the opposite side of the fence (presumably the border of a neighbouring country) asking him to pass the ball back. Hesitating to talk with a person (presumably an enemy), he looks back to see if his parents are watching. After thinking for a while, the boy kicks the ball towards the other who, in turn, invites him over to join the game. Not minding the restrictions any more, the boy crosses the boundary and joins his new friend. They start playing together and the voiceover concludes, "Deewarein gir jaati hain, faasle mit jaate hain, jahan do baatein ho jaati hain (Barriers break when people talk)." The TVC ends with Airtel's signature tune.[2]

The war-torn territory idea was decided as the best basis to bring forth this thought, as barriers of two kinds are broken - communication barriers and, subsequently, the borders of the two warring countries. The campaign uses children as symbols of minds- free of prejudice, with their innocence depicted in stark contrast to the desolate landscape around them. Airtel's point of view has clearly become this: The world would be a better place if only we all talked to each other.[2]

3. *Google Search – Reunion*: Reunion is a 2013 Google India advertisement for Google Search. It was directed by Amit Sharma, written by Sukesh Kumar Nayak, produced by an Ogilvy India (branch of Ogilvy & Mather) and published on YouTube on November 13, 2013. Singer Clinton Cerejo composed its music.

The TVC portrays the reunion of two elderly men, Baldev Mehra from India and Yusuf from Lahore, Pakistan. They were separated as children during the Partition of India. Baldev shows his granddaughter Suman an old photograph of two children. He tells her that it is of him and his best friend Yusuf when they lived in Lahore before the Partition of India in 1947. In front of his house there was a park with a gate made in the stone age. Each evening he and Yusuf would fly kites there and steal jhajariyas from Yusuf's family sweet shop. However, when Partition was announced, Baldev and his family had to leave for India overnight. The commercial portrays that Baldev still thinks of Yusuf and misses him many decades later.

Using details of her grandfather's story, Sumon is able to locate Yusuf's sweet shop in Lahore via 'Google Search'. She connects with his grandson Ali who helps her to plan a surprise visit from Yusuf on Baldev's birthday.[3]

It has had a strong impact in both India and Pakistan. It went viral and was viewed more than 1.6 million times before officially debuting on television on November 15, 2013.[4]

Sukesh Kumar Nayak, Group Creative Director of Ogilvy Mumbai expressed that the company wanted was to see how meaningful the search engine is in real life; thereby making the connection between real life and Google, magical.[3]

India Today states that the TVC touches the raw nerves that linger dormant under the skin of those who were separated during the Partition.

Nilanjana Bhowmick of *Time Observes* said that despite the tensions between the two governments, this advertisement makes the point that the personal connections between the two countries run deep.[5]

Ritu Singh of Zee News states that the TVC struck an emotional chord with its viewers from both the countries as it depicts the pain of partition which still haunts the mind of people who got separated from their loved ones and places.[6]

Mrigaa Sethi of Quartz talking about her family's experience with partition, noted that the commercial has struck a particularly emotional chord by refusing to take the historically adversarial relationship between the two countries as a given.[7]

Abhijit Avasthi, head of the Ogilvy India team that developed the TVC, revealed that one of the reasons for choosing the idea was the fact that partition evokes strong feelings among both the countries but the purpose was to tell people that those bitter memories are in the past and that there is a way to revive your lost connection.[8]

4. *Coca-Cola– Small World Machines (Open Happiness)*

Coca-Cola had released a TVC in 2013 featuring a campaign that takes the brand's 'Open happiness' proposition forward across borders.

The advertisement showcases a pair of connected vending machines that Coke and the agency (Leo Burnett) set up in India and Pakistan. Each vending machine featured a webcam and a giant touch screen monitor. Passers by could grant free cold-drinks to the people on the other side of the digital window by participating in a series of simple joint activities like – wave, touch hands, draw a peace sign or dance with each other. The TVC portrays that what unites us is stronger than what sets us apart by inviting consumers to put their differences aside and share a moment over a Coke.

Jackie Jantos Tulloch, who led the project, noted that the brand Coca-Cola is powerful enough because of the voice and scale of the brand, but when the brand is layered with a story like this on top, it goes beyond just telling a Coca-Cola story but telling a bigger, more profound story about the connectedness of the world.

Andy DiLallo, chief creative officer, Leo Burnett Sydney said that they dealt with time differences, language barriers and cultural sensitivities but seeing a little kid run up to the machine and try to high-five and another person saying that he lived in India his entire life and had never 'seen into' Pakistan, made everything worth.[9]

Saad Pall, Assistant Brand Manager for Coca-Cola in Pakistan noted that the people from both the countries share a lot of common passions and interests, from food and Bollywood movies, to Coke Studio music, to cricket. The TVC connected people who are not exposed to each other on a daily basis, enabling the common man in Lahore to see and interact with the common man in Delhi.

Ajay Naqvi, general manager, creative excellence, Coca-Cola India, said he got goosebumps the first time he saw the film as he realised that cultural and social tensions exist around the world for selfish reasons but deep down humanity is about togetherness and happiness. [10]

Wasim Basir, integrated marketing communications director, Coca-Cola India, said that we wondered what would happen if people from these two countries came together, and the answer was clear: goodness and happiness."[11]

5. *Fevikwik – Todo nahi, Jodo*

Fevikwik (Pidilite Industries) unveiled its TVC campaign titled Fevikwik 'Todo Nahin, Jodo' with the India vs. Pakistan match during World Cup, 2015. The TVC subtly weaved in the brand attributes of Fevikwik as an instant adhesive promoting the broader message of strengthening bond between people.

The film opens at an arched gate. One soldier each from both sides (presumingly India and Pakistan) is seen marching. Each is trying to outdo the other, and as they go through their marching routine it is noticed that the shoe sole of one of the soldiers (Pakistani) has peeled off. Fearing a loss-of-face, as crowds look on, he looks appealingly at his rival on the other side (Indian). The Indian soldier waves his arms about in a flurry of movement following which the shoe is shown as being fixed. A slow motion replay reveals that the Indian soldier had pulled out a tube of Fevikwik and mended the shoe instantly, the action hidden by the speed of his movements. The march continues and the soldiers salute each other at which point, a Super appears on screen while a voice over is also heard saying –"Fevikwik. Todo nahin, Jodo!"

Vivek Sharma, Chief Marketing Officer, Pidilite Industries Ltd, said that the TVC elevates the brand attribute of bonding from a functional to emotional level. TVC takes a witty perspective on human bonding combining Fevikwik's instant adhesion quality with Pidilite's tradition of using humour in its advertising,

Piyush Pandey, Executive Chairman & Creative Director, South Asia-O&M commented on the campaign saying that the product is about solving problems, bonding and about bringing a smile on the face of everyone in the world.[12]

6. *Kohinoor Basmati Rice – True Taste Unites*

The TVC was launched on the eve of Independence Day, 2015. The commercial weaves a budding modern love story of an Indian boy from Delhi and a Pakistani girl from Lahore showcasing how both India and Pakistan, despite the border hostilities, are united in several similar tastes, one of them being the taste for Kohinoor Basmati Rice. The boy and the girl meet at their office in New York. There are differences at the beginning but when they both reach for a packet of Kohinoor at a store, they begin to realise that they are not so different after all and it acts as an ice-breaker.[26]

Conceptualised by Crayons Advertising, Delhi, the TVC portrays how the friendship between an Indian boy and a 'not so friendly' Pakistani girl blossoms over biryani cooked with the advertised product. Directed by Ravi Jain of Venus Productions, the film revolves around the age old comparison between the two countries.

Ranjan Bargotra, President, Crayons Advertising, speaking on the creative insight behind the film, said that the film is aimed at the Indian diaspora settled overseas wherein it has been observed that people from both Pakistan and India have the greatest bonding, despite whatever rivalries that the countries have. The nationalities get blurred in a foreign country and we are seen as one community.[13]

Rondeep Gogoi, Creative Director, Crayons Advertising, Delhi, explains that the TVC portrays the tag line of the brand (True Taste Unites) perfectly as brand plays cupid and brings the two people together.[13]

KV Sridhar, Chief Creative Officer, Sapient Nitro believes that the intent was good and the idea was a beautiful one, however, he felt that the India-Pakistan theme had been overused in brand communication.[13]

Harish Bijoor of Harish Bijoor Consults, echoing similar views said that a story of bonding through a common brand is a cliché today and managing this cliché is a matter of high skill; but the execution in this particular TVC was missing. [13]

Saurabh Dasgupta, Executive Creative Director, Innocean expressed that first of all the TVC tries to bridge India and Pakistan, which is a much bigger agenda than selling rice. It attempts a larger good than just selling great quality rice; and secondly, the commercial tackles the perception that while people from both the countries may think that they are different, but at different levels they are similar. [13]

7. *Nestle EveryDay – Ye Hai Kuch Khaas – Celebrating 150 Years*

The TVC showcased India and Pakistan may be at tussle for almost everything but, deviating from the usual, the company Nestle, in its 2016 'EveryDay' TVC, brought together ace Indian tennis player Sania Mirza and her Pakistani cricketer husband Shoaib Malik to agree. The commercial portrays how Shoaib and Sania loved the stuff of their own country. She prefers Amritsar's sweet (laddoo), he thinks Multan's sweet (soan halwa) is better. She likes old Hindi songs, while he prefers Pakistan pop songs. She swears by Shimla's winter weather, but for Shoaib, nothing beats Islamabad's rain. But they finally end their truce when their frustrated domestic help serves them tea and the couple, in a turnaround, instantly agree that Nestle EveryDay is the best choice for making a perfect cup of tea.[14]

Advertising related Laws/Codes in India

The Government of India has not set up a regulatory body in India to regulate advertisements. But as in due course depending on the nature of the grievances, the power to regulate advertisements may be exercised by a vast variety of authorities, including the courts, Central and state governments, tribunals or the police authorities. In addition to that, numerous legislations also deal with advertisement provisions in part, unfortunately, though not in total. (Refer Annexure - IV for the list of laws, rules and regulations that deal with advertisements.)

But in the cases related to promotion of international peace and harmony; only the following laws/codes count:

1. *Constitution of India*:

Article 19 (1) (a) of the Constitution of India states that all citizens shall have the right to freedom of speech and expression.

Article 19 (2) of the Constitution of India states that nothing in sub clause (a) of clause (1) shall affect the operation of any existing law, or prevent the State from making any law, in so far as such law imposes reasonable restrictions on the exercise of the right conferred by the said sub clause in the interests of the sovereignty and integrity of India, the security of the State, friendly relations with foreign States, public order, decency or morality or in relation to contempt of court, defamation or incitement to an offence.

2. *The ASCI Code*

Standards of conduct – Clause III states that no advertisement shall be permitted which: Tends to incite people to crime or to promote disorder and violence or intolerance, derides any race, caste, colour, creed or nationality, presents criminality as desirable or directly or indirectly encourages people - particularly minors - to emulate it or conveys the modus operandi of any crime or adversely affects friendly relations with a foreign State.

3. *Press Council of India – Norms of Journalistic Conduct*

Article 24. Foreign Relations: Media plays a very important role in moulding public opinion and developing better understanding between countries. Objective reporting so as not to jeopardise friendly bilateral relations is therefore desirable.

Article 25. Newspapers may expose misuse of diplomatic immunity: The media shall make every possible effort to build bridges of cooperation, friendly relations and better understanding between India and foreign States. At the same time, it is the duty of a newspaper to expose any misuse or undue advantage of the diplomatic immunities.

4. *Doordarshan – Code for Commercial Advertising*:

General rules for conduct in advertising:

1. Advertising shall be so designed as to conform to the laws of the country and shall not offend the morality, decency and the religious susceptibilities of the people.
2. No advertisement shall be permitted which adversely affects friendly relations with foreign countries.

5. *Programme and Advertising Codes –The Cable Television Network Rules, 1994*:

Rule 6. Programme Code (1) No programme should be carried in the cable service which:- (a) Offends against good taste or decency; (b)

Contains criticism of friendly countries; (c) Contains attack on religions or communities or visuals or words contemptuous of religious groups or which promote communal attitudes.

Apart from the above stated ones, most of the Indian laws, rules, codes or norms outrightly mention that no advertisement shall contain criticism of friendly countries; and that they would not jeopardise peace and harmony of the country.

Conclusion

India and Pakistan have a very peculiar relationship, which oscillates between peace and discord. The antagonisms that divide India and Pakistan are real, but there is also the reality of common ties, heritage and attachments. Unfortunately, if the people of the two countries have grown apart, it is partly because the people have ceased to know one another.

Many Bollywood movies have been made highlighting the conflicts between India and Pakistan. Some of the well known ones are Hindustan Ki Kasam (1973), Aakraman (1975), Vijeta (1982), Param Vir Chakra (1995), Border (1997), LOC Kargil (2003), Deewaar (2004), Lakshya (2004), 1971 (2007), Tango Charlie (2005) and War Chhod Na Yaar (2013).[15]

Zee Entertainment Enterprises Ltd launched Zindagi channel which brought Pakistan's TV content closer to Indians in 2014.[16]

In February 2016 Film makers from both the countries have had also come up together in an initiative called as the, 'Zeal for Unity' which is a peace initiate taken by both the countries in a joint effort to spread harmony among its people. In the midst of political controversies between India and Pakistan, six Indian directors and six Pakistani directors are coming together on a common platform for an apolitical exchange to mark the onset of the 70th year of the country's Partition. From Pakistan, the six directors who have made the films are Mehreen Jabbar, Sabiha Sumar, Khalid Ahmed, Shahbaz Sumar, Siraj Ul Haq and Meenu Farjad. And from India, there are Aparna Sen, Tanuja Chandra, Ketan Mehta, Nikhil Advani, Tigmanshu Dhulia and Bejoy Nambiar. This is a momentous step towards changing the way people across India and Pakistan see, feel and think about each other.[16]

All the above mentioned case studies portray that conflict is not the only interaction between the two countries. The two countries are just like next-door neighbours who might quarrel but also feel proud of the shared similarities they enjoy. Everything, including the culture, culinary habits and traditions of both the countries are in harmony with each other, except for its people. Being obsessed by the contradictions, we give more emphasis on them than to our similarities. To mend this we must distinguish between real and apparent contradictions.

Dissemination of cultural resemblances will provide a broader understanding of our rich tradition and aesthetics. And to bring these similarities to the forefront; a few multi-national companies have conceptualised the trend of innovative television advertisements with an underlying message of love and harmony that exists in the hearts of the citizens of both the countries – India and Pakistan.

Such advertisements can go a long way in promoting peace and harmony between both the countries as can be seen from the overwhelming response the advertisements have received from the citizens of both the states. Such strong emotions among the people can have a bold impact on the government policies and actions.

References

1 *The Generals - 8pm Whisky TV Commercial Ad.* (n.d.). Retrieved from http://www.advertolog.com/radico-khaitan/adverts/the-generals-1156005/

2 *Airtel breaks barriers to break the clutter.* (n.d.). Retrieved from http://www.afaqs.com/news/story/20051_Airtel-breaks-barriers-to-break-the-clutter

3 *Reunion (advertisement).* (n.d.). Retrieved from https://en.wikipedia.org/wiki/Reunion (advertisement)

4 *Emotional Google ad a viral hit in India and Pakistan* - World - CBC News. (n.d.). Retrieved from http://www.cbc.ca/news/world/emotional-google-ad-a-viral-hit-in-india-and-pakistan-1.2427935

5 *World Overnight: Why Indians and Pakistanis Find This Ad Incredibly Moving.* (n.d.). Retrieved from https://punditfromanotherplanet.com/2013/11/14/world-overnight-why-indians-and-pakistanis-find-this-ad-incredibly-moving/

6 *Reunion Google Advert Goes Viral.* (n.d.). Retrieved from www.ashugaur.com/reunion-google-advert-viral/

7 *Google's Plan to Win Over Indians—by Making Them Cry* - The Atlantic. (n.d.). Retrieved from http://www.theatlantic.com/international/archive/2013/11/googles-plan-to-win-over-indians-by-making-them-cry/281496/

8 *Viral video: Google ad connects India-Pak with heartwarming reunion story* | Page 11. (n.d.). Retrieved from http://defence.pk/threads/viral-video-google-ad-connects-india-pak-with-heartwarming-reunion-story.287264/page-11

9 *Coca-Cola tries to unite India and Pakistan with interactive vending machines that encourage users in both countries to 'make a friend'* | Daily Mail Online. (n.d.). Retrieved from http://www.dailymail.co.uk/indiahome/indianews/

article-2330617/Coca-Cola-tries-unite-India-Pakistan-interactive-vending-machines-encourage-users-countries-make-friend.html

10 *Coca-Cola Small World Machines: The Coca-Cola Company.* (n.d.). Retrieved from http://www.coca-colacompany.com/stories/happiness-without-borders

11 *Coca-Cola tries to unite India and Pakistan with interactive vending machines that encourage users in both countries to 'make a friend'* | Daily Mail Online. (n.d.). Retrieved from http://www.dailymail .co.uk/indiahome/indianews/article-2330617/Coca-Cola-tries-unite-India-Pakistan-interactive-vending-machines-encourage-users-countries-make-friend.html

12 *Fevikwik Todo Nahi Jodo | Ads Watcher.* (n.d.). Retrieved from http://adswatcher.blogspot .in/2015/04/fevikwik-todo-nahi-jodo.html

13 *Kohinoor Basmati Rice – When boundaries divide, but taste unites | Best Media Info, News and Analysis on Indian Advertising, Marketing and Media Industry.* (n.d.). Retrieved from http://www.bestmediainfo.com/2015/08/kohinoor-basmati-rice-when-boundaries-divide-but-taste-unites/

14 *Sania Mirza and Shoaib Malik indulge in Indo-Pak banter in Nestle EveryDay Ad.* (n.d.). Retrieved from http://www.afaqs.com/news/story/47429_Sania-Mirza-and-Shoaib-Malik-indulge-in-Indo-Pak-banter-in-Nestle-EveryDay-Ad

15 Indo-Pakistani wars and conflicts. (n.d.). Retrieved from https://en.wikipedia.org/wiki/Indo-Pakistani_wars_and_conflicts

16 *In 'zeal for unity', Indian, Pakistani filmmakers to bridge divide* | The Indian Express. (n.d.). Retrieved from http://indianexpress.com/article/entertainment/entertainment-others/in-zeal-for-unity-indian-pakistani-filmmakers-to-bridge-divide/

9

Advertising Vis-A-Vis LGBT's Human Rights

Homosexuality in India had been banned under Section 377 of the Indian Penal Code, 1860; thereby making homosexual sex punishable by law. To many Indians the idea of same-sex relationships is unknown, even alien. This has been just one outcome of British imperialism and Victorian prudery or morality (a distillation of the moral views of people living at the time of Queen Victoria's reign between 1837 to 1901 and of the moral climate of the regions she ruled upon including India); they negated our indigenous cultures and histories by drawing a veil between our present from the past.[1] However, homosexuality has a history in this country. It has been documented that references of homosexuality have been found in texts written in 15 Indian languages over a period of more than 2000 years that challenge the stereotype that Indian tradition has always been too conservative/puritan to allow any homoerotic exploration.[2] Homosexuality also finds reference in texts like 'Arthashastra' which is an ancient Indian treatise on statecraft. 'Arthashastra' mentions a wide variety of homosexual practices which sought to be punished with the lowest grade of fine.[3]

Eventually, the British government banned homosexual relations under Section 377 of the Indian Penal Code, 1860. This made it an offence for a person to voluntarily have 'carnal intercourse against the order of nature.'[4]

There are no official demographics for the LGBT population in India, but the government of India submitted figures to the Supreme Court in 2012, according to which, there were about 2.5 million gay people recorded in India. These figures are only based on those individuals who have self declared to the Ministry of Health. There may be much higher statistics for individuals who have concealed their identity, since a number of homosexual Indians are living in the closet due to fear of discrimination.[5]

This law was struck down by the 2009 Delhi High Court decision in Naz Foundation v. Govt. of NCT of Delhi, which found Section 377 and other legal prohibitions against same-sex conduct to be in direct violation of fundamental rights provided by the Indian Constitution.

Decisions of a High Court on the constitutionality of a law (i.e. judicial review) apply throughout India, and not just to the territory of the state over which the High Court in question has jurisdiction.[6] However, even after the pronouncement of verdict, there have been few incidents of harassment of homosexual groups.[7]

On 16 February 2012, the Supreme Court, during a hearing of a bunch of appeals filed against decriminalisation of gay sex, observed that homosexuality should be seen in the context of changing society as many things which were earlier unacceptable have become acceptable with passage of time.

The two-judge bench, composed of Justices G S Singhvi and S J Mukhopadhaya, opined that homosexuality should be seen in the light of changing times where phenomena of live-in relationship, single parents and artificial fertilisation have become normal. They had also pointed out that many things, which were considered immoral 20 years ago, have become acceptable to society now. The bench said that gay sex was not an offence prior to 1860 and referred to paintings and sculptures of Khajuraho. Senior Advocate Amrendra Sharan, who opposed the Delhi High Court order of decriminalising gay sex on behalf of the Delhi Commission for Protection of Child Rights, had then submitted that social issues cannot be decided on the basis of sculptures. The apex court bench, however, observed that it is a reflection of society of that time and homosexuality should not be seen only in terms of sexual intercourse. Earlier, the Supreme Court bench had asked the anti-gay rights groups, challenging legalisation of gay sex, to explain how such acts are against the order of nature as submitted by them.

The apex court was hearing petitions filed by anti-gay rights activists and also by political, social and religious organisations which have opposed the Delhi High Court verdict decriminalising homosexual behaviour.

However, on 23rd of February 2012, the Union Home Ministry of the UPA government replying on a Supreme Court observation, told the apex Court that it was opposed to the decriminalisation of gay sex as it was highly immoral and against the social order. It said that India's moral and social values were different from other countries, and therefore, the nation should not be guided by them.[8] The Central Government reversed its stand on 28th of February 2012, asserting that there was no error in decriminalising gay sex. This resulted in the apex court pulling up the Centre for frequently changing its stand on the issue. Don't make a mockery of the system and don't waste the court's time, an apex court judge told the government.[9]

Also in 2012, a guide titled 'Creating Inclusive Workplaces for LGBT employees in India' was developed by IBM, Goldman Sachs, Google together with Community Business, a non-profit organization.[10]

In December 2013, however, the Supreme Court upheld the law that criminalises gay sex, in a ruling that reverses a landmark 2009 Delhi High Court order which had decriminalised homosexual acts. The court said it was up to parliament to legislate on the issue.

The protests against the reinstitution of Section 377 took place across India, and resulted in political activism across political parties to declare their support for the law's repeal. By April 2014, which was the time of the upcoming election, at least three major political parties - the Aam Aadmi Party, the Congress and the Communist Party of India (Marxist) - had included support for decriminalization of homosexual relations in their election manifestos, while the BJP's leadership supported the law.[3]

Coming-outs and Pride Parades

In 2005, Prince Manvendra Singh Gohil, who hails from Rajpipla in the Gujarat, publicly came out as gay. He was quickly anointed by the Indian and the world media as the first openly gay royal. He was disinherited as an immediate reaction by the royal family, though they eventually reconciled. He appeared on the American talk show 'The Oprah Winfrey Show' on October 24th 2007,[11] and 'Undercover Princes' on BBC Three.[12]

On 29 June 2008, five Indian cities (Delhi, Bangalore, Kolkata, Indore and Pondicherry) celebrated gay pride parades. About 2,000 people turned out in these nationwide parades.

Days after the 2 July 2009 Delhi High Court verdict legalising homosexuality, 'Pink Pages', India's first online LGBT magazine was released.[13] On 16th April 2009, India's first gay magazine 'Bombay Dost' originally launched in 1990, was re-launched by Celina Jaitley in Mumbai.[14]

On 27th June 2009, Bhubaneswar, the capital city of Odisha, saw its first gay pride parade.[15] A day later, the then Union Law Minister Veerappa Moily announced that the Union Home Minister has convened a meeting with the Union Law Ministers, Union Health Ministers and Home Ministers of all states to evolve a consensus on decriminalising homosexuality in India.[16] On 28th June 2009, Delhi and Bangalore held their second gay pride parades, and Chennai, generally considered to be a very conservative city, held its first.[17,18]

Mumbai has one of its own pride events, like 'Kashish Mumbai Queer Film Festival' which was first held in the year 2010 from 22nd to 25th

April[19] and in the next year 2011 from 25th to 29th May.[20] It was the first queer film festival in India and is held in a mainstream multiplex theatre which screens LGBT films from all over the world.[21]

Madurai celebrated city's first LGBTQ Rainbow festival on 29th July 2012. Anjali Gopalan inaugurated Alan Turing Rainbow festival and flagged off the Asia›s first Gender queer pride parade as a part of Turing Rainbow festival organised by Srishti Madurai, a literary and resource circle for alternative gender and sexualities. It was established by Gopi Shankar, a student of 'The American College in Madurai' to eradicate social discrimination faced by the LGBT and Genderqueer community. The objective of the organisation is to highlight twenty different types of genders.[22,23]

On 1st of May 2011, 'Kolkata Rainbow Pride Festival' (KRPF) was formed to take the initiative of organising 'Pride Walk' in Kolkata. Since then, the initiative of 'Queer Pride Parade' in Kolkata is being taken by KRPF. The 11th Kolkata Rainbow Pride Walk, held on 15th July 2012, was attended by more than 1500 people.[24] Kolkata hosted South Asia›s first pride walk in the year 1999.

Chandigarh held its first LGBT pride parade on 15th March 2013 and it has been held annually ever since.

The first LGBT pride parade in Gujarat state was held at Surat on 6th October 2013.[25]

Rajasthan witnessed its first pride event on 1th March 2015, when a pride walk was held in Jaipur.[26]

In the year 2013, India was represented by Nolan Lewis, a model, at the Mr Gay World 2013 contest. He had trouble finding sponsors. Previously, India had been represented at the Mr Gay World by Zoltan Parag Bhaindarkar in the year 2008. He did not return to India and reportedly sought asylum in the United States.[27]

Sushant Divgikar, the winner of Mr Gay India 2014, was a contestant on the 'Bigg Boss' reality show.[28] On 26th July 2014, at Kochi the 5th All-Kerala Queer Pride Parade was held.[29] It was organised by Queerala (a support group for the LGBT community) and Sahayathrika (a rights organisation for lesbian and bisexual women in Kerala).[30]

In July 2014, the first book on 'Genderqueer' in Tamil and the first Tamil book on LGBTQIA by Srishti Madurai was released by BJP's state general secretary Vanathi Srinivasan at the 6th Hindu spiritual service foundation's sixth service fair, Chennai.[31] In June 2016, a platform named 'AMOUR Queer Dating' (www.amourqueerdating.blogspot.in) is launched in India, to help queer/LGBTIQ people find long term companions. [32,33,34]

Case Studies

Positive Advertisements

1. *Fastrack* - *'Come out of the closet...Move on'*: Accessories brand Fastrack launched a commercial that ruffled a few feathers with its LGBT (lesbian, gay, bisexual and transgender) theme. The TVC, which became an instant Internet sensation, opened with a shot of a trembling closet. But instead of a man and a woman, two girls emerged from the closet and looked at each other meaningfully while the tagline read: 'Come out of the closet...Move on.'[35]

Fastrack's tight connect with the youth segment is attributed largely to the brand's edgy and provocative advertising campaigns.[36] Walking an extremely thin line between irreverent and insolent, Fastrack's radical commercials manage to grab eyeballs with their youth-oriented focus.

The 2013 campaign revolves around challenging societal conventions, as an extension of its 'move on' philosophy. The mood is set by graphic visuals, Daft Punk music, and subtle suggestion.[37]

2. *eBay* - *'#ThingsDontJudge'*: eBay India has a new advert running online, as well as on television, with an interesting and thought-provoking theme called #ThingsDontJudge.[38] The central idea is that things or products, inherently, don't carry with it any kind of judgement or bias based on gender, age, religion, sexual orientation and other identity markers.

Now, while it may be easy to dismiss this as a typical, Hollywood-centric, 'no judgement' drama, eBay forces us to rethink how we view assumptions about certain acts. The ad implies that judgement has got nothing to do with the things itself, but only people who attach certain negative connotations to it. Connotations for an object develop over time and eBay seeks to deconstruct that in 70 seconds.

If 'Ghungroos', mobile phones, and rings could speak, would they tell a man to not dance, pout, or love another man? Will a 'Salwaar Kameez' ridicule a lady bike rider as 'behenji'? No, they won't. A reclining chair won't question a housewife taking rest, nor would 'Khan' as a surname prevent 'Aamna' (name known from the nameplate shown in the advertisement) from celebrating Diwali.[39]

So, why not turn towards these inanimate objects - 10 crore of them, which don't judge - asks a new ad by the e-commerce marketplace eBay. Conceptualised by BBDO India, the television-led campaign

#ThingsDon'tJudge talks about various situations where people are seen breaking away from prejudices that the society imposes on them.

In a significant move for LGBTQ visibility, a man is seen proposing to his male partner with a silver ring with the background narration saying, "*A ring is supposed to denote my love.*" By clearly stating the object (the ring) with the denotation (to express love), it manages to leave out judgemental connotations (love only defined in hetero-normative terms i.e. between a man and a woman). Many wondered whether this portion of the advertisement would be cut out for television since an earlier ad by Myntra based on a lesbian couple was never shown. But to the surprise of many, it has been retained.[38]

The whole act of separating denotation from connotation is a significant cultural move and it is hard to depict that on television, which eBay seems to have done with relative ease.

3. *Jabong – 'Be you'*: Jabong's latest campaign is a contemporary take on the brand's positioning of 'Be You'. The TVC portrayed men wearing bridal nose rings along with heels and girls wearing green lipsticks with turbans. The brand attempts to break the clichés of fashion by being bold by featuring men and women in various unorthodox and gender-bending outfits and accessories.[40]

Genderfluidity or the ability to fluctuate between two or more genders, is somewhat an esoteric part of the gender spectrum.[41] Genderfluidity is often confused with being transgender or intersex, and thus, the discussion around the topic has been woefully non-existent.

The commercial has been conceptualised by Bates CHI & Partners, with renowned London-based award-winning photographer and artistic director Harvey B. Brown behind the cameras.

The brand is reiterating the idea of individuality to inspire and encourage the youth of India to be comfortable in their skin.[42] The TVC which is aired across channels, has been innovatively shot across many cities in India, capturing the personal styles of youngsters, and emotions derived from the sense of empowerment and confidence from fashion, the commercial showcases the latest styles and trends across clothes, shoes and accessories.

Praveen Sinha, Founder and MD, Jabong.com said that the brand is constantly innovating itself to churn out something new for its customers and this time they are not merely promoting clothes, but a concept that never goes out of fashion.[42]

Negative Advertisements

1. ***Virgin mobile – 'Think hat ke':*** A girl tells her parents, "Mom Dad mujhe aapse kuch kehna hai" (Mom Dad I need to tell you something). "Bolo" (Say). After a brief pause she says, "Mujhe ladko me koi interest nahi hai" (I am not interested in boys). When her mom asks her the meaning of what she is saying; all she says is 'meaning?' suggesting that she is a lesbian. Her parents immediately starts blaming each other of their decisions to send her to a girl's school and of not letting her mix with the boys of the building. Then a boy calls her up, but she says she is not interested and hangs up. On being questioned by the father as who the caller was; she curtly replies no one but just a friend from MBA class who was making plans to visit Goa. She also emphasized that she was not interested. But her father was insisting that she should go as she must participate in co-curricular activities. Her mother protested as his name sounded like 'Tensing'. But the father snapped her saying that atleast he is a boy; thus he will be good. Thus the tagline goes, 'Jab life dilaye jhatke; soch zara hatke' (When life shocks you, think differently). The TVC ends with her calling up her male friend and saying, "Tensing, Goa is on".

Herein, she does not out rightly tell them that that she is a lesbian. She just says that she does not have any interest in boys on purpose to make them fear what she might be turning into; making them regret their actions to keep her away from boys in the past and thereby, allowing her to go to Goa with her male friend.[43]

This advertisement is negative as it only highlights the fact that homosexuality is a taboo; and also the patriarchal belief that a person, just because he is a boy, will be good.

2. ***Pepsi– 'Youngistan ka wow':*** This Pepsi Youngistan ad features Ranbir Kapoor. The situation is rather funny: a boy has come to see a girl, and Pepsi is served; a marriage negotiation is on the cards. The girl is rather reluctant to marry. Suddenly, Ranbir comes out from nowhere and kisses the would-be-groom on the cheeks. The guy is flabbergasted, the parents shocked, and the girl is delighted. The suitor really does not know Ranbir and he says so; immediately another guy materializes from an adjacent room and asks the would-be-groom sadly whether he would also deny knowing him. The negotiation is broken off immediately and the girl thanks the boys for the drama. But they say they are there for the Pepsi; not to help her.[44]

The advocates of the advertisement believe that the little drama that Ranbir conjures up is surprisingly without any hidden mockery at homosexuals per se. The theme of the ad is totally in tune with the pranks Ranbir, with a characteristic naughtiness, is usually seen to play on others. Somehow one is bound to feel that after all some kind of naturalness is attributed to the possibility of homosexual affairs. However, the appearance of the second guy who also claims to be in a relationship with the would-be-groom underscores the polygamous nature of homosexual people. This is a kind of essentialization, no doubt. But, in a way, it also underscores the positive possibility of being in more than one relationship at the same time. The morality associated with heterosexual marriage and monogamy is overturned very subtly. However, the interpretation of this may vary. Some may look upon the introduction of the second guy as a disapproving commentary on the promiscuous nature of gay men. However, this may be read down by drawing attention to the fact that Youngistan wants more and still more...their desires are insatiable. Such desire is not only confined to the material realm of gadgets, food or fashion, but also effortlessly extends to the emotional world. So promiscuity or multiple affairs have become the order of the day, and are not specific only to same-sex relationships.[45]

But the people having contrary views believe that the advertisement also highlights the fact that homosexuality is a taboo in the Indian society. Thus, to break the proposal the best way was to fix the suitor as a homosexual as it was a sure-shot way to dissuade the parents from letting their girl marry him.

Advertisements – Other than TVCS

Big Brands openly show their support for LGBT community.

1. ***Anouk*:** While advertising in India is still quite conventional, Anouk - a clothing brand that retails on on-line store Myntra.com is making sure it breaks stereotypes. This touching new ad shows a conversation between a lesbian couple, like any other. It beautifully captures the nervousness, excitement and anxiousness of a girl introducing her partner to her parents. The lightness and casualness of the conversation and the intonation of dialogues brings out the message of equality like no other. Love has no gender, and more so as the ad rightly says 'And I don't wanna hide it anymore'.[46] Indian netizens have welcomed the ad and social media is abuzz with support for the campaign. A part of Anouk's 'bold is beautiful' campaign this one titled 'The Visit' may just trigger a new era in social advertising and it only gets better from here.[47]

2. ***Allen Solly***: Allen Solly, an apparel brand belonging to the Aditya Birla group on its official facebook page changed its cover image to the rainbow colours with the text 'All Colors Were Created Equal #Sec 377'.[48]
3. ***Amul***: The Anand Milk Union Limited is famous for using puns on current affairs. This time, it utilized the 'Amul girl' mascot laying flowers on the grave and the headstone bearing the engraving 'Freedom of Choice – 2013'.[48]
4. ***Tanishq***: Jewellery brand Tanishq, which is owned by Titan, a Tata group company, on its twitter page, uploaded an ad which showed a pair of diamond earrings with the words "Two of a kind always make a beautiful pair! #sec 377". Previously, Tanishq had supported the cause of remarriage of women. [48]
5. ***Hidesign:*** The luxurious handbags brand also mixed its marketing and the cause with the poster showing the rainbow colours at the bottom and placing the bag of that shade on that colour shade. The caption was 'Every Colour, Every Shape, Every Size is Beautiful. In a World Full of Diversities we are Equal', and under the colour shade, in the centre '#377' was written. [48]
6. **UrbanClap:** Mobile services marketplace 'UrbanClap' has released a digital ad film in the year 2016 in support of India's Lesbian-Gay-Bi-sexual-Trans-gender (LGBT) community.[49] The film is about a young homosexual girl whose father has a hard time accepting reality. Interestingly, a rebel in his era, the said father married a Muslim girl - the protagonist's mother - despite societal opposition, back in the day. The catchphrase is 'Capture your love - come out in support of true love'. The brand urges members of the LGBT community to 'come out' for a photo shoot.

   For this campaign, UrbanClap worked with a Delhi-based startup agency called 'Ufaan', that has worked on films around similar themes in the past.[50]

   Says the brand team on its YouTube page: "With this film UrbanClap hopes that all of us will acknowledge the fact that every love deserves its special place in the world. So, come out for your photo shoot & capture your love with #pride! We at 'UrbanClap' are a simple bunch of people. We believe that everyone should have the right to love whoever they want to - in many ways; it's the most basic human right. We stand firmly by the side of the LGBT community in India, as they fight for their equal rights, in the eyes of the law, or society.

Our past efforts with the Naz Foundation (an NGO that supports the cause of sexual health), and this film, are very small gestures towards furthering the cause of the Lesbian, Gay, Bi-sexual and Trans-gender (LGBT) community. As part of this effort, we are also giving away free photoshoots to LGBT community couples. The easiest way to reach out to us is to tag UrbanClap on Facebook or Twitter, with the hashtag #Comeoutforyourphotoshoot..."[49]

7. ***Red Label:*** Brooke Bond Red Label is positioned as the 'tea that brings people together' and this is beautifully encapsulated in the promise 'Swaad apnepan ka' (Taste of affinity). It promises that the world could be a more welcoming place if one can put aside prejudices and accept others in the spirit of friendship and brotherhood.[51]

   The campaign was launched in January 2016 with six trans-genders and six videos over six months. The songs spoke the language of Red Label. Its debut song 'Hum Hai Happy' (We are happy), based on Pharrell William's hit 'Happy', sets the tone of the campaign. The song recounts its philosophy of being happy, despite the adversity.

   In the company blog, Shiva Krishnamurthy, General Manager, Beverages, Hindustan Unilever, said, "We wanted to create new content for our brand that meaningfully engaged our customers with our brand's purpose – to make the world a more welcoming place, one cup of tea at a time. We wanted a campaign that expressed our brand values, that went beyond tokenism or photo opportunities, something daring and provocative that tackled taboos. This is what attracted us to the idea pitched by the youth arm of Yash Raj Films – Y Films – which saw us creating an ad with a band of transgender musicians called the 6-Pack Band."[49]

8. ***Red Lotus*:** An Indian fashion designer is aiming to break down stereotypes by using transgender women to model her latest collection. Designer Sharmila Nair, from Cochin in the southern Indian state of Kerala, has named her new line of saris 'Mazhavil', which means rainbow. "Since the LGBT community is represented by the rainbow flag, I thought why not give my collection the same shades and use all the colours of the rainbow." Nair said.[52]

9. ***Myntra*:** One of India's largest online shopping destination for fashion and lifestyle products, Myntra has over 1.6 million fans on Facebook. A few days late, but Myntra did come up with a smart visual on its Facebook page that incorporated the letter 'M' from its logo. The poster had M+W, M+M and W+W with the tagline 'Get this straight Don't discriminate'.[53]

Advertising related Laws in India

The Government of India has not set up a regulatory body in India to regulate advertisements. But, as in due course depending on the nature of the grievances, the power to regulate advertisements may be exercised by a vast variety of authorities, including the courts, Central and state governments, tribunals or the police authorities. In addition to that, numerous legislations also deal with advertisement provisions in part, unfortunately, though not in total. (Refer Annexure - IV for the list of laws, rules and regulations that deal with advertisements.) But only the following talk of rights of LGBT:

1. *Constitution of India:*

a. Article 15 of the Indian Constitution prohibits the State from discriminating against any citizen on grounds only of religion, race, caste, ***sex***, place of birth or any of them.
b. Article 21 of the Indian Constitution reads that no person shall be deprived of his life or personal liberty except according to procedure established by law.

2. *Indian Penal Code, 1860*

Section 377 of the IPC deals with punishment for unnatural offences. It reads: whoever voluntarily has carnal intercourse against the order of nature with any man, woman or animal shall be punished with imprisonment for life, or with imprisonment of either description for term which may extend to ten years, and shall also be liable to fine.

3. *The ASCI Code*

Chapter – III of the ASCI states that no advertisement shall be permitted which derides any race, caste, colour, creed, gender or nationality.

4. *Press Council of India – Norms of journalistic conduct*

Avoid references to caste, gender or sexual orientation and not to reinforce stereotypes about sexual minorites including those who are lesbian, gay, bisexual or transgender (LGBT).

Apart from the above stated ones, most of the Indian laws, rules, codes or norms outrightly mention that no advertisement shall contain criticism of friendly countries; and that they would not jeopardise peace and harmony of the country.

Conclusion

Since it has been observed that there is a global awareness regarding the acknowledgment of the LGBT community; it is natural that Indian advertisers are also deciding to vouch for their rights. Here, probably the advertisers are making optimum use of the right to freedom of speech and expression, guaranteed under Article 19 (1)(a) of the Constitution of India. But, that what has been criminalized by the Indian law; should no way be proliferated by the citizens of the country or any part thereof which includes the brands, their advertisers or other relevant components of the same.

At the same time, it is difficult for us to say if the Supreme Court judgment of 2013 will continue to be in vogue forever. There is a provision that the Supreme Court can review its own judgment; and with the kind of awareness and public pressure that has been seen to gradually manifest in the favour of the LGBT community, there might come a time and situation where the Supreme Court will also give a judgment in the favour of the community.

The researcher personally supports the view that every citizen of the country, however natural or unnatural they are in their outlook, should enjoy equal rights under the Constitution of India. Being a lesbian, gay or bi-sexual are mere sexual orientations; and a very private concern of an individual. This cannot be a criterion to judge people if they should be given their legitimate rights or not. Whatever an individual does in his private sphere should not be anybody's concern as long as it does not harm public interest. Even the LGBT community has their right to privacy; which should not be encroached upon.

Our Indian constitution talks of non-discrimination based on caste or gender but, the Indian Penal code still clings on to Section 377; thereby revealing that the word 'gender' in the constitution only means male or female. Thus, it is time that we broaden the radius of the word 'gender' and even include trans-genders in its meaning; giving them the right to equality, privacy and personal liberty.

At this juncture, it will be very difficult to say if the awareness for the LGBT rights is ethically right or wrong. The stand of the researcher here is that the advertisement campaigns are ethically right but legally wrong as the rights of the LGBT community constitute a very important part within the vast gamut of human rights; but, since India does not sanction the same legally; the outright promotion of the same is not advisable. Though it is hoped that such advertisements go a long way in finally giving justice to the minority community and they too, under the Article 21 of the Indian constitution, can lead a life with personal freedom and liberty.

References

1 *Queer India: Gay historians: Ruth Vanita and Saleem Kidwai.* (n.d.). Retrieved from http://queerindia.blogspot.in/2005/03/gay-historians-ruth-vanita-and-saleem.html

2 Burkhart, G. (2003). Same-Sex Love in India: Readings from Literature and History. Edited by Ruth Vanita and Saleem Kidwai. New York: St. Martin's Press, 2000. 352 pp. $55.00 (cloth). *The Journal of Asian Studies, 62*(01), 322-323. doi:10.2307/3096220

3 *LGBT history of India.* (n.d.). Retrieved from https://en.wikipedia.org/wiki/LGBT _history_of_India

4 *Law Commission of India.* (n.d.). Retrieved from lawcommissionofindia.nic.in/1-50/report42.pdf

5 *India has 2.5m gays, government tells supreme court* - BBC News. (n.d.). Retrieved from http://www.bbc.com/news/world-asia-india-17363200

6 *Some HC judges are becoming terribly ignorant of our Constitution!.* (n.d.). Retrieved from http://www.legallyindia.com/Blogs/some-hc-judges-are-becoming-terribly-ignorant-of-our-constitution

7 *Crackdown on gay party in Saharanpur, 13 held - Times of India.* (n.d.). Retrieved from http://timesofindia.indiatimes.com/india/Crackdown-on-gay-party-in-Saharanpur-13-held/articleshow/7175530.cms

8 *Homosexuality: Govt opposes HC verdict in apex court.* (n.d.). Retrieved from http://www.mumbaimirror.com/article/3/20120223201202231413279 34d025428/Homosexuality-Govt-opposes-HC-verdict-in-apex-court.html

9 *Supreme Court pulls up Centre for flip-flop on homosexuality - Indian Express.* (n.d.). Retrieved from http://www.indianexpress.com/news/supreme-court-pulls-up-centre-for-flipflop-on-homosexuality/917743/?google_editors_picks=true

10 *Lesbian, gay, bisexual and transgender resource guide for employers* - Times of India. (n.d.). Retrieved from http://timesofindia.indiatimes.com/india/Lesbian-gay-bisexual-and-transgender-resource-guide-for-employers/articleshow/16739968.cms

11 *India's gay prince appears on Oprah show.* (n.d.). Retrieved from http://www.rediff.com /news /2007/oct/26look1.htm

12 *BBC Three - Undercover Princes.* (n.d.). Retrieved from http://www.bbc.co.uk/programmes/b00gtkyq

13 *Rainbow Chronicles* | The Indian Express. (n.d.). Retrieved from http://indianexpress.com /article/cities/kolkata/rainbow-chronicles/

14 *Celina re-launches pro-gay mag Bombay Dost:* News18 Videos. (n.d.). Retrieved from http://www.news18.com/videos/india/celina-bombay-dost-313986.html

15 *Maiden rainbow pride walk* - The Telegraph - Calcutta (Kolkata). (n.d.). Retrieved from http://www.telegraphindia.com/1090628/jsp/nation/story_11167322.jsp

16 *Centre won't rush Sec 377 repeal, says Moily* - Rediff.com India News. (n.d.). Retrieved from http://www.rediff.com/news/report/not-rushing-gay-law-repeal-moily/20090628.htm

17 *City prepares for gay pride march [Chennai]* | Queer Media Watch: India. (n.d.). Retrieved from https://qmediawatch.wordpress.com/2009/06/20/city-prepares-for-gay-pride-march-chennai/

18 *Gay activists rejoice over Centre's plan, hold parades* - Times of India. (n.d.). Retrieved from http://timesofindia.indiatimes.com/india/Gay-activists-rejoice-over-Centres-plan-hold-parades/articleshow/4713107.cms

19 *Celebrate 7 Shades of Love at Kashish Mumbai International Queer Film Festival.* (n.d.). Retrieved from www.dnaindia.com/locality/news-tags/kashish-mumbai-international-queer-film-festival

20 *LGBT film festival kick starts second edition in Mumbai.* (n.d.). Retrieved from www.dnaindia.com/entertainment/report-lgbt-film-festival-kick-starts-second-edition-in-mumbai-1547650

21 *Queer films from Pakistan, Iran head for Kashish.* (n.d.). Retrieved from www. dnaindia.com /entertainment/report-queer-films-from-pakistan-iran-head-for-kashish-1834780

22 *Madurai comes out of the closet - The Hindu.* (n.d.). Retrieved from http://www.thehindu. com/news/cities/Madurai/madurai-comes-out-of-the-closet/article3702689.ece

23 *Worldwide gay rights as a social movement picks up.* (n.d.). Retrieved from www.merinews.com/article/worldwide-gay-rights-as-a-social-movement-picks-up/15914647.shtml

24 *Pride parade breaks record.* (n.d.). Retrieved from http://www.telegraphindia.com /1120716/jsp/calcutta/story_15733112.jsp

25 *First gay parade held in India's Gujarat state* - Telegraph. (n.d.). Retrieved from http://www.telegraph.co.uk/news/worldnews/asia/india/10360598/First-gay-parade-held-in-Indias-Gujarat-state.html

26 *Pride walk: LGBT group demands social, economic rights* | Jaipur | Hindustan Times. (n.d.). Retrieved from http://www.hindustantimes.com/jaipur/pride-walk-lgbt-group-demands-social-economic-rights/story-cVx2yZzg9Bbz9ubtzho0uJ.html

27 *Proud to be Out* | *Tehelka.* (n.d.). Retrieved from http://www.tehelka.com/2013/08/proud-to-be-out/

28 *Bigg Boss contestant Sushant Divgikar hopes to sensitise TV viewers to LGBT cause - Times of India.* (n.d.). Retrieved from http://timesofindia.indiatimes.

com/tv/news/hindi/Bigg-Boss-contestant-Sushant-Divgikar-hopes-to-sensitise-TV-viewers-to-LGBT-cause/articleshow/43251775.cms

29 *Queer Pride march in Kochi - KERALA - The Hindu.* (n.d.). Retrieved from http://www.thehindu.com/todays-paper/tp-national/tp-kerala/queer-pride-march-in-kochi/article6253916.ece

30 *Fifth Kerala LGBT parade pride held* - DNA India. (n.d.). Retrieved from www.dnaindia.com/india/report-fifth-kerala-lgbt-parade-pride-held-2005667

31 *It's a great honour to be awarded for book on gender variants: Gopi Shankar - Times of India.* (n.d.). Retrieved from http://timesofindia.indiatimes.com/city/madurai/Its-a-great-honour-to-be-awarded-for-book-on-gender-variants-Gopi-Shankar/articleshow /38769130.cms

32 *Amour - A dating platform for Queer.* (n.d.). Retrieved from http://amourqueerdating. blogspot.in/

33 *Now, a dating platform for LGBT community.* (n.d.). Retrieved from www.dnaindia.com/mumbai/report-now-a-dating-platform-for-lgbt-community-2236832

34 *'Amour'- A Brand New Dating Platform For Queer Indians. – GayIndia.* (n.d.). Retrieved from https://gayrightsindia.wordpress.com/2016/07/21/amour-a-brand-new-dating-platform-for-queer-indians/

35 *Brands flirt with taboo topics in TV ads - Times of India.* (n.d.). Retrieved from http://timesofindia.indiatimes.com/business/india-business/Brands-flirt-with-taboo-topics-in-TV-ads/articleshow/25337309.cms

36 *The prince of cool - Titan Industries - Tata group.* (n.d.). Retrieved from http://www.tata.in /article /inside/v4wVshbcNL8=/TLYVr3YPkMU=

37 *Titan Fastrack: Come out of the closet... Move on.* (n.d.). Retrieved from https://www.youtube .com /watch?v=yJe9fEx7u58

38 *New eBay Ad Shows Gay Couple, Breaks Stereotypes On Gender, Age And Religion.* (n.d.). Retrieved from http://www.youthkiawaaz.com/2016/10/ebay-ad-breaking-stereotypes/

39 *Men can pout, dance in ghungroos, be gay; Don't judge: eBay India's new spot.* (n.d.). Retrieved from http://www.afaqs.com/news/story/49092_Men-can-pout-dance-in-ghungroos-be-gay-Dont-judge-eBay-Indias-new-spot

40 *Advertising & Marketing Industry News* - AdAge. (n.d.). Retrieved from http://www.adageindia. in/advertising/harvey-b-brown-creates-jabongs-new-campaign/articleshow/52556240.cms

41 *Jabong's New Ad Celebrates Genderfluidity In All Its Glory.* (n.d.). Retrieved from http://www.feminisminindia.com/.../video-jabongs-new-ad-celebrates-genderfluidity-glory/

42 *Jabong launches 'Be You' campaign.* (n.d.). Retrieved from http://www.exchange4media. com/advertising/jabong-launches-be-you-campaign_57474.html

43 *Virgin Mobile India Think Hatke Funny TV Commercial Ad #1.* (n.d.). Retrieved from https://www.youtube.com/watch?v=5FUIqPPlMd0

44 *Ranbir Kapoor - Pepsi TVC 2010.* (n.d.). Retrieved from https://www.youtube.com /watch?v=IJyMtoENWZ0

45 *Kaustav's Arden: Two recent television ads and 'gay' sites of sexual ambivalence.* (n.d.). Retrieved from http://kaustavsarden.blogspot.in/2010/10/two-recent-television-ads-and-gay-sites.html

46 *Anouk's ad featuring a lesbian couple has a powerful message for India | Latest News & Updates at Daily News & Analysis.* (n.d.). Retrieved from http://www.dnaindia.com/lifestyle/ video-anouk-s-ad-featuring-a-lesbian-couple-has-a-powerful-message-for-india-2094505

47 *Anouk's ad featuring a lesbian couple has a powerful message for India - GenX i Social Buzz.* (n.d.). Retrieved from http://www.genxisocialbuzz.com/index.php/anouks-ad-featuring-a-lesbian-couple-has-a-powerful-message-for-india/

48 *Brands That Say, "It's Okay To Be Gay" - Youth Connect.* (n.d.). Retrieved from http://www.youthconnect.in/2013/12/18/brands-that-say-its-okay-to-be-gay/

49 *UrbanClap supports Lesbian-Gay-Bisexual-Transgender community in new ad.* (n.d.). Retrieved from http://www.afaqs.com/news/story/48160_UrbanClap-supports-Lesbian-Gay-Bisexual-Transgender-community-in-new-ad

50 *UrbanClap launches campaign addressing LGBTQ issues | Indian Television Dot Com.* (n.d.). Retrieved from http://www.indiantelevision.com/mam/media-and-advertising/ad-campaigns/urbanclap-launches-campaign-addressing-lgbtq-issues-160603

51 *Brooke Bond Red Label's 6-Pack Band: How it became a story worth watching again and again | Best Media Info, News and Analysis on Indian Advertising, Marketing and Media Industry.* (n.d.). Retrieved from http://www.bestmediainfo.com/2016/08/brooke-bond-red-labels-6-pack-band-how-it-became-a-story-worth-watching-again-and-again/

52 *Indian Fashion Brand Red Lotus Uses All Transgender Models For New Sari Campaign | Huffington Post.* (n.d.). Retrieved from http://www.huffingtonpost.co.uk/entry/transgender-indian-models_uk_5745cc40e4b02163fae84e38

53 *11 Indian Brands Support The LGBT Community On Facebook Amidst SC's #Sec377 Ruling | Lighthouse Insights.* (n.d.). Retrieved from http://lighthouseinsights.in/11-indian-brands-support-the-lgbt-community-on-facebook-amidst-scs-sec377-ruling.html/

10

Conclusion

Television in India was first experimented in the year 1959 but regular transmission was introduced only in 1965. It was only in the year 1972 that television service was extended to two major cities –Mumbai and Amritsar. However, it was not until the mid-seventies (1974 and 1975) that national television service and 'Doordarshan' were available in the major cities of the country. Hence, it was considered appropriate to conduct a content analysis of commercials in or after 1974 to get the correct perspective of the transition that happened after the 1991 Economic reforms which led to liberalisation, privatisation and globalisation in India. Thus, the case studies range from the year 1970s to 2016. The study presents content analysis of 78 advertisements out of which 69 are television commercials; and the rest are portrayals of similar themes in other media of mass communication like that of newspapers, magazines or the internet. The content analysis focuses on the human rights factors underlying the advertisements; and if the current laws and regulations have been able to cater to the needs of the problems arising out of such communication. Opinion from 97 expert interviews have been included in the research work.

This Chapter, hence, provides answers to the research questions briefly presenting the results of the content analysis; making sure that the study has been conducted according to the objectives set out in the introductory chapter. The chapter also includes the recommendations for improvement of the television advertising and the Indian legal scenario with respect to the human rights perspective.

The content of various Indian television advertisements have been critically analyzed and their violations/representations of various laws, norms, codes of ethics or regulations have been highlighted with reference to the Human Rights angle. Television advertisements have been sorted under wider areas of Human rights and analyzed if they have followed the laws and ethics of the country.

The present advertising codes of conducts have been thoroughly studied to see if the relevant points in context of human rights are being catered to by them. The various International Conventions and the laws of our land regarding Human Rights have been studied to see if there is any mention of violation of rights in context of the topic of our study.

Findings with Reference to Advertising related Laws in India

In Part A of Chapter – III, after taking an in-depth look at all the laws and codes relating to both advertisements and also to the protection of the rights of the child, we have come to the conclusion that no Code of conduct manual relating to advertisements express explicitly that the rights of the child need to be preserved. There is no mention of the rights to privacy, self esteem and dignity of the child. There is no mention that the child portrayed through advertisements should not be shown in a derogatory manner.

In Part B, it has been observed that the Government of India has not set up a regulatory body in India to regulate advertisements related to privacy of women in context of portraying them in a derogatory way. But, depending on the nature of the grievances, the power to regulate advertisements may be exercised by a vast variety of authorities, including the courts, Central and state governments, tribunals or the police authorities. In addition to that numerous legislations also deal with advertisement provisions in part not in total unfortunately. There are almost twenty-four rules, regulations and legislations in the country with respect to advertisements but only two of them - The ASCI Code and the 'Indecent Representation of Women (Prohibition) Act, 1986' that deal with privacy of women.

In Part A of Chapter – IV, it has been observed that India has a very few legislations to govern advertisements as far as the obscenity is concerned. Section 292 of the Indian Penal Code, 1860; Section 6 of the Cable television networks rules, 1994 and the Indecent Representation of Women Prohibition Act, 1987 are the only three laws out of almost 24 rules, laws, codes and regulations in India that deal with advertisements.

In Part B, it has been observed that out of all the advertisement related laws and ethics in India only the Constitution of India; the ASCI Code; Consumer Protection Act, 1986; The Drugs and Cosmetics Act, 1940; The Indecent Representation of Women (Prohibition) Act, 1986 and the Cable Television Networks (Regulation) Act deal with various aspects of colour discrimination in Indian advertisements.

In Part A of Chapter – V, it has been observed that despite the fact that India has ample number of legislations, rules, regulations and norms related to advertising ethics only a few of them deal with promotion of communal harmony. Some of these laws and regulations are Articles 19, Article 25(1), Article 28 and Article 51A(h) of the Indian Constitution,

Section 153A and Section 295(A) of the Indian Penal Code, The ASCI, Press Council of India – Norms of Journalistic Conduct, Doordarshan – Code for Commercial Advertising and the Programme and Advertising Codes –The Cable Television Network Rules, 1994.

In Part B, it has been found that only five laws, rules and regulations out of the various legislations, rules, regulations and norms related to advertising ethics in India are relevant in context of promotion of international peace and harmony. These laws and regulations include the Constitution of India, the ASCI Code, Press Council of India – Norms of Journalistic Conduct, Doordarshan – Code for Commercial Advertising and the Programme and Advertising Codes –The Cable Television Network Rules, 1994.

In Part A of Chapter – VI, it has been observed that despite the fact that India has ample number of legislations, rules, regulations and norms related to advertising ethics only a few of them deal with LGBT. These laws and regulations include the Constitution of India, the ASCI Code and the Press Council of India – Norms of Journalistic Conduct.

Tabular Representation of the Analysis

Sr. No	*Advertising related laws/ rules/codes*	*RTP of Child*	*RTP of Women*	*Lascivious*	*Colour dis-crimi-nation*	*Communal harmony*	*India & Pak*	*LGBT*
1	Constitution of India	✓	×	×	✓	✓	✓	✓
2	Advertising Standards Council of India (ASCI)	✓	✓	✓	✓	✓		✓
3	Indecent Representation of Women (Prohibition) Act	×	✓	✓	✓	×	×	×
4	Consumer Protection Act	×	×	×	✓	×	×	×
5	The Drugs and Cosmetics Act	×	×	×	✓	×	×	×
6	Cable Television Networks (Regulation) Act	×	×	×	✓	×	×	×

7	Cable television networks rules	✓	✓	✓	×	✓	✓	×
8	Press Council of India's Norms for Journalistic ethics	✓	✓	×	×	✓	✓	✓
9	Indian Penal Code	×	×	✓	×	✓	×	×
10	Code of Criminal Procedure	×	×	×	×	✓	×	×
11	Code for commercial advertising (DD)	×	✓	×	×	×	✓	×

Apart from the above mentioned laws, there are many other media related laws that we have mentioned in our various chapters. They also deal with advertisement provisions in part, but unfortunately, not in total. (Refer Annexure E for the list of laws, rules and regulations that deal with advertisements.) Unfortunately, none of these laws talk about the human rights aspect in the parlance of our topics of study.

Recommendations

1. Organisation in support of human rights of different sections of people should take the matter of any such violations through television advertisements seriously; and bring it to light, so that public and authorities concerned can take necessary actions.
2. The NGOs should put pressure on the advertising companies to take the human rights angle into notice. The NGOs along with public should put pressure on the government to take the matter into notice and initiate the process of proper legislations on the matter.
3. From the above tabular representation, it is evident that, apart from ASCI, there are no specific legislations governing advertising in India, but even ASCI is not up to the mark to govern advertising spectrum. ASCI should be made a stronger body by vesting in it certain statutory powers. Considering that seventy-five percent of the advertising sector is regulated by ASCI as well as the fact that the Cable Television Networks (Amendment) Rules, 2006 stipulates that all the advertisements will have to abide by ASCI's Code for Self-Regulation in Advertising. It is

suggested that ASCI should, in fact, be given certain binding powers, however, it does not mean that ASCI would be elevated to the position of state.

ASCI should also be given the power to screen the advertisements before they are aired on television so that the advertisements offending good public taste are not broadcast at the first place.

Apart from this, there should be a robust mechanism which deters the advertisers to air offensive advertisements. ASCI should be conferred the power to impose binding financial sanctions, the amount of which should be reasonably high to deter various advertisers and advertising agencies.

4. All the Codes and norms relating to advertising standards should be amended and those provisions that would protect the rights of privacy, self esteem and dignity should be inserted. It is evident that all that is needed is a codified uniform legislation as Advertising Laws.
5. We should also have laws like the Indecent Displays (Control) Act 1981 which is an Act of Parliament covering Scotland, England and Wales. It is concerned with preventing the display of 'indecent' material to the unsuspecting public. The Act does not define indecency, although it does give some directions as to how a display can be considered indecent. It establishes that 'if any indecent matter is publicly displayed, the person making the display and any person causing or permitting the display to be made, shall be guilty of an offence'.
6. We should also have laws like the Indecent Advertisements Prohibition Act, 1963 that is enforced in Bangladesh. It defines:
   (a) 'advertisement' includes any notice, circular or other document, displayed on any house, building or wall, or published in any newspaper or periodical, and any announcement made orally or by any means of producing or transmitting light or sound, but does not include trade circulars issued by manufacturers of drugs to medical practitioners.
   (b) 'indecent' includes whatsoever may amount to any incentive to sensuality and excitement of impure thoughts in the mind of an ordinary man of normal temperament, and has the tendency to deprave and corrupt those whose minds are open to such immoral influence, and which is deemed to be detrimental to public morals and calculated to produce pernicious effect, in depraving and debauching the minds of persons.

7. We should have such laws that are binding on both the producers and advertisers of the products. Unless the laws are strict, advertisers will not be cautious regarding their violations of other's rights.
8. It is also the duty of the aware citizens and institutions like judiciary to raise their voice through Public Interest Litigations against airing of such advertisements on national television.
9. Under the Cable Television Networks (Regulation) Act, the ministry issues directions to television channels or cable TV operators to stop airing an advertisement and not to the advertisers. But unless the advertisers are booked and given penalty, the menace of such advertisements would be seen more than often in national television.
10. Philanthropic institutions should understand their duties and responsibilities well and should go out to all minimum extent to protect the weak and the vulnerable sections of the society for which they are set up. These organizations should not shy away from their responsibilities.
11. It should be the collective responsibility of the client, the consumer, the channel and the creative agency to ensure that an immoral, derogatory, objectionable material does not go out.
12. However, there is a possibility that those big advertisers and advertising agencies which annually earn huge amount of profit would easily bypass such a system of financial sanctions and would keep airing obscene advertisements. To check such advertisers, the ASCI should be linked with criminal courts which can impose criminal sanctions on such advertisers showing recurring public interest violations in their advertisements. There should be a swift linkage between ASCI and courts, wherein the former can take the blameworthy advertisers to the courts and get them punished.
13. It is suggested that not only the advertisers who come up with obscene advertisements, but also the television channels which screen such advertisements should be deemed culpable and be subsequently punished. If such suggestions are taken into account and ASCI is made a stronger body, we can regulate the television advertisements; thereby, substantially curbing the ill-effects of obscene advertising in the Indian society.
14. Lastly, it is suggested that even if obscenity is an extremely vague and subjective concept, the yardstick that of a 'reasonable man' should be used to deal with determination of obscenity in advertisements.

Thus, it is seen that there are perspectives in Indian advertising scenario, where human rights have been infringed in the rat race to catch consumer attention.

Secondly, there are very little stringent measures to protect some 'significant; yet, not taken notice' of angles of human rights of certain sections of the society. Moreover, there are no defined authorised bodies to monitor the ethical weightage of advertisements, especially the ones aired on television. The provisions of the Constitution of India, too, are not all-encompassing. There are void zones in the Indian legal system. The advertisers reap benefits of these void zones.

Various perspectives of human rights violations through these void zones, first has to be felt, then objected by writing against them. Then, through a series of reasonable debates, the presence of this void is established. The government, through the Parliament, enacts pertinent laws and the Supreme Court issues relevant orders to clear the area of void. Every important law in this world regarding protection of racial discrimination, animal life, ecology and others, have come into force because of the writings of aware citizens.

The researcher has discussed and highlighted various laws related to our area of research that are in execution in different countries of the world. It is a humble suggestion that necessary laws be enacted in India too for the protection of human rights of the referred group of people in our society.

The research helped us find that even though India has different laws relating to advertisements but, unfortunately, they are yet to transcend from the print advertisements to television; or to further newer forms of media like the internet. For example, the Information Technology Act, 2000 was enacted in India as it was noticed that the existing Indian Penal Code was insufficient to cater to the needs of the new crimes emerging from the internet expansion. But, the effort was incomplete until the definition of 'Electronic record' was inserted as Section 29A in the 'Indian Penal Code, 1860'.

Thus, it can be observed that when a new law is enacted, it is required that much of the already existing laws are also amended; but, in our country there is a void in this aspect. For instance, the 'Indecent representation of the women Act' does not synchronize with the non-punitive codes mentioned by ASCI. Legal system has to metamorphose with the ongoing transformation and evolution of the society. Even a similar law on 'Indecent representation of children or LGBT' is yet to come.

Erring units hamper the healthy growth of the society. One cannot expect peace, progress and stability when one section of the society, advertently or inadvertently, keeps underestimating any other section of the society. So, it is required that the erring units must be brought to book. The most important step in this direction could be submission of an affidavit by all advertisers that they would stand by the 'golden rules of human rights' and would no way display anything (whether in spoken, written, signs, signals or any other visual representation), through their advertisements, that would mean violation of the same.

A book is the best platform wherein the seeds of such ideas can sowed and put forward to the reading audience. Hence, it is hoped that the effort will go a long way in bringing the required changes in the ethical front of Indian television advertising scenario.

Annexure I

The Code for Self-Regulation in Advertising

ASCI Goals:

1. To monitor, administer and promote standards of advertising practices in India with a view to:
   (i) ensuring the truthfulness and honesty of representations and claims made through advertising and safeguarding against misleading advertising.
   (ii) ensuring that advertising is not offensive to generally accepted norms and standards of public decency.
   (iii) safeguarding against the indiscriminate use of advertising for the promotion of products or services which are generally regarded as hazardous to society or to individuals or which are unacceptable to society as a whole.
   (iv) ensuring that advertisements observe fairness in competition and the canons of generally accepted competitive behaviour.
2. To codify, adopt and from time to time modify the code of advertising practices in India and implement, administer and promote and publicize such a code.
3. To promote, maintain and uphold fair, sound, ethical and healthy principles and practices of advertising.
4. To promote better understanding of the benefits of fair, sound and ethical advertising amongst the practitioners of advertising and in society at large.
5. To represent, protect, inform and guide the members of the company on matters relating to advertising.
6. To foster and promote co-operation amongst persons or companies engaged and involved in advertising.

Purpose:

The purpose of the code is to control the content of advertisements, not to hamper the sale of products which may be found offensive, for whatever reason, by some people. Provided, therefore, that advertisements for such products are not themselves offensive, there will normally be no ground for objection to them in terms of this code.

Declaration of Fundamental Principles:

This Code for Self-Regulation has been drawn up by people in professions and industries in or connected with advertising, in consultation with representatives of people affected by advertising, and has been accepted by individuals, corporate bodies and associations engaged in or otherwise concerned with the practice of advertising, with the following as basic guidelines, with a view to achieve the acceptance of fair advertising practices in the best interest of the ultimate consumer:

I. To ensure the truthfulness and honesty of representations and claims made by advertisements and to safeguard against misleading advertisements,

II. To ensure that advertisements are not offensive to generally accepted standards of public decency,

III. To safeguard against the indiscriminate use of advertising for the promotion of products which are regarded as hazardous to society or to individuals to a degree or of a type which is unacceptable to society at large,

IV. To ensure that advertisements observe fairness in competition so that the consumer's need to be informed on choices in the market-place and the canons of generally accepted competitive behaviour in business are both served.

The Code's rules form the basis for judgement whenever there may be conflicting views about the acceptability of an advertisement, whether it is challenged from within or from outside the advertising business. Both the general public and an advertiser's competitors have an equal right to expect the content of advertisements to be presented fairly, intelligibly and responsibly. The Code applies to advertisers, advertising agencies and media.

Responsibility for the observance of this code:

The responsibility for the observance of this Code for Self-Regulation in Advertising lies with all who commission, create, place or publish any advertisement or assist in the creation or publishing of any advertisement. All advertisers, advertising agencies and media are expected not to commission, create, place or publish any advertisement which is in contravention of this code. This is a self-imposed discipline required under this Code for Self-Regulation in Advertising from all involved in the commissioning, creation, placement or publishing of advertisements. This code applies to advertisements read, heard or viewed in India even if they originate or are published abroad so long as they are directed to consumers in India or are exposed to significant number of consumers in India.

The Code and the law:

The Code's rules are not the only ones to affect advertising.

There are many provisions, both in the common law and in the statutes, which can determine the form or the content of an advertisement. The code is not in competition with law. Its rules and the machinery, through which they are enforced, are designed to complement legal controls, not to usurp or replace them.

Definitions:

For the purpose of this code:

- an advertisement is defined as a paid-for communication, addressed to the public or a section of it, the purpose of which is to influence the opinions or behaviour of those to whom it is addressed. Any communication which in the normal course would be recognised as an advertisement by the general public would be included in this definition even if it is carried free-of-charge for any reason.
- a product is anything which forms the subject of an advertisement, and includes goods, services and facilities.
- a consumer is any person or corporate body who is likely to be reached by an advertisement whether as an ultimate consumer in the way of trade or otherwise.
- an advertiser is anybody, including an individual or partnership or corporate body or association, on whose brief the advertisement is designed and on whose account the advertisement is released.
- an advertising agency includes all individuals, partnerships, corporate bodies or associations, who or which work for planning, research, creation or placement of advertisements or the creation of material for advertisements for advertisers or for other advertising agencies.
- media owners include individuals in effective control of the management of media or their agents; media are any means used for the propagation of advertisements and include press, cinema, radio, television, hoardings, hand bills, direct mail, posters, internet, etc.

- minors are defined as persons who are below the age of 18 years.
- any written or graphic matter on packaging, whether unitary or bulk, or contained in it, is subject to this Code in the same manner as any advertisement in any other medium.
- to publish is to carry the advertisement in any media whether it be by printing, exhibiting, broadcasting, displaying, distributing, etc.

Standards of conduct:

Advertising is an important and legitimate means for the seller to awaken public interest in his products. The success of advertising depends on public confidence. Hence, no practice should be permitted which tends to impair this confidence. The standards laid down here should be taken as minimum standards of acceptability which would be liable to be reviewed from time to time in relation to the prevailing norm of consumers' susceptibilities.

The ASCI code for self regulation has been divided into four chapters; which are mentioned as follows:

Chapter-I: TRUTHFUL & HONEST REPRESENTATION

To ensure the truthfulness and honesty of representations and claims made by advertisements and to safeguard against misleading advertisements -

1. Advertisements must be truthful. All descriptions, claims and comparisons which relate to matters of objectively ascertainable fact should be capable of substantiation. Advertisers and advertising agencies are required to produce such substantiation as and when called upon to do so by 'The Advertising Standards Council of India'.
2. Where advertising claims are expressly stated to be based on or supported by independent research or assessment, the source and date of this should be indicated in the advertisement.
3. Advertisements shall not, without permission from the person, firm or institution under reference, contain any reference to such person, firm or institution which confers an unjustified advantage on the product advertised or tends to bring the person, firm or institution into ridicule or disrepute. If and when required to do so by the 'Advertising Standards Council of India', the advertiser and the advertising agency shall produce explicit permission from the person, firm or institution to which reference is made in the advertisement.
4. Advertisements shall neither distort facts nor mislead the consumer by means of implications or omissions. Advertisements shall not contain statements or visual presentation which directly or by implication or

by omission or by ambiguity or by exaggeration are likely to mislead the consumer about the product advertised or the advertiser or about any other product or advertiser.

5. Advertisements shall not be so framed as to abuse the trust of consumers or exploit their lack of experience or knowledge. No advertisement shall be permitted to contain any claim so exaggerated as to lead to grave or widespread disappointment in the minds of consumers.

For example:

(a) Products shall not be described as `free' where there is any direct cost to the consumer other than the actual cost of any delivery, freight, or postage. Where such costs are payable by the consumer, a clear statement that this is the case shall be made in the advertisement.

(b) Where a claim is made that if one product is purchased, another product will be provided 'free', the advertiser is required to show, as and when called upon by 'The Advertising Standards Council of India', that the price paid by the consumer for the product which is offered for purchase with the advertised incentive is no more than the prevailing price of the product without the advertised incentive.

(c) Claims which use expressions such as 'Upto five years' guarantee' or 'Prices from as low as Rs. Y' are not acceptable if there is a likelihood of the consumer being misled either as to the extent of the availability or as to the applicability of the benefits offered.

(d) Special care and restraint has to be exercised in advertisements addressed to those suffering from weakness, any real or perceived inadequacy of any physical attributes such as height or bust development, obesity, illness, impotence, infertility, baldness and the like, to ensure that claims or representations directly or by implication, do not exceed what is considered prudent by generally accepted standards of medical practice and the actual efficacy of the product.

(e) Advertisements inviting the public to invest money shall not contain statements which may mislead the consumer in respect of the security offered, rates of return or terms of amortisation; where any of the foregoing elements are contingent upon the continuance of or change in existing conditions, or any other assumptions, such conditions or assumptions must be clearly indicated in the advertisement.

(f) Advertisements inviting the public to take part in lotteries or prize competitions permitted under law or which hold out the prospect of gifts shall take clearly all material conditions as to enable the consumer to obtain a true and fair view of their prospects in such activities. Further, such advertisers shall make adequate provisions for the judging of such competitions, announcement of the results and the fair distribution of prizes or gifts according to the advertised terms and conditions within a reasonable period of time. With regard to the announcement of results, it is clarified that the advertiser's responsibility under this section of the Code is discharged adequately if the advertiser publicizes the main results in the media used to announce the competition as far as is practicable and advises the individual winners by post.

6. Obvious untruths or exaggerations intended to amuse or to catch the eye of the consumer are permissible provided that they are clearly to be seen as humorous or hyperbolic and not likely to be understood as making literal or misleading claims for the advertised product.
7. In mass manufacturing and distribution of goods and services it is possible that there may be an occasional, unintentional lapse in the fulfilment of an advertised promise or claim. Such occasional, unintentional lapses may not invalidate the advertisement in terms of this Code.

   In judging such issues, due regard shall be given to the following:

   (a) Whether the claim or promise is capable of fulfilment by a typical specimen of the product advertised.
   (b) Whether the proportion of product failures is within generally acceptable limits.
   (c) Whether the advertiser has taken prompt action to make good the deficiency to the consumer.

Chapter-II: NON-OFFENSIVE TO PUBLIC

To ensure that advertisements are not offensive to generally accepted standards of public decency.

Advertisements should contain nothing indecent, vulgar, especially in the depiction of women, or nothing repulsive which is likely, in the light of generally prevailing standards of decency and propriety, to cause grave and widespread offence.

Chapter-III:
AGAINST HARMFUL PRODUCTS / SITUATIONS

To safeguard against the indiscriminate use of Advertising in situations or of the promotion of products which are regarded as hazardous or harmful to society or to individuals, particularly minors, to a degree or of a type which is unacceptable to society at large.

1. No advertisement shall be permitted which:
   (a) Tends to incite people to crime or to promote disorder and violence or intolerance.
   (b) Derides any race, caste, colour, creed, gender or nationality
   (c) Presents criminality as desirable or directly or indirectly encourages people - particularly minors - to emulate it or conveys the modus operandi of any crime.
   (d) Adversely affects friendly relations with a foreign State.
2. Advertisements addressed to minors shall not contain anything, whether in illustration or otherwise, which might result in their physical, mental or moral harm or which exploits their vulnerability. For example, advertisements:
   (a) Should not encourage minors to enter strange places or to converse with strangers in an effort to collect coupons, wrappers, labels or the like.
   (b) Should not feature dangerous or hazardous acts which are likely to encourage minors to emulate such acts in a manner which could cause harm or injury.
   (c) Should not show minors using or playing with matches or any inflammable or explosive substance; or playing with or using sharp knives, guns or mechanical or electrical appliances, the careless use of which could lead to their suffering from cuts, burns, shocks or other injury.
   (d) Should not feature minors for tobacco or alcohol-based products.
   (e) Should not feature personalities from the field of sports, music and cinema for products which, by law, either require a health warning in their advertising or cannot be purchased by minors.
3. Advertisements shall not, without justifiable reason, show or refer to dangerous practices or manifest a disregard for safety or encourage negligence.
4. Advertisements should contain nothing which is in breach of the law nor omit anything which the law requires.

5. Advertisements shall not propagate products, the use of which is banned under the law.
6. Advertisements for products whose advertising is prohibited or restricted by law or by this Code must not circumvent such restrictions by purporting to be advertisements for other products the advertising of which is not prohibited or restricted by law or by this Code. In judging whether or not any particular advertisement is an indirect advertisement for a product whose advertising is restricted or prohibited, due attention shall be paid to the following:
   (a) Whether the unrestricted product which is purportedly sought to be promoted through the advertisement under complaint is produced and distributed in reasonable quantities having regard to the scale of the advertising in question, the media used and the markets targeted.
   (b) Whether there exist in the advertisement under complaint any direct or indirect clues or cues which could suggest to consumers that it is a direct or indirect advertisement for the product whose advertising is restricted or prohibited by law or by this Code.
   (c) Where advertising is necessary, the mere use of a brand name or company name that may also be applied to a product whose advertising is restricted or prohibited, is not reason to find the advertisement objectionable provided the advertisement is not objectionable in terms of (a) and (b) above.

Chapter-IV: FAIR IN COMPETITION

To ensure that advertisements observe fairness in competition such that the consumer's need to be informed on choice in the market-place and the canons of generally accepted competitive behaviour in business are both served.

1. Advertisements containing comparisons with other manufacturers or suppliers or with other products including those where a competitor is named, are permissible in the interests of vigorous competition and public enlightenment, provided:
   (a) It is clear what aspects of the advertiser's product are being compared with what aspects of the competitor's product.
   (b) The subject matter of comparison is not chosen in such a way as to confer an artificial advantage upon the advertiser or so as to suggest that a better bargain is offered than is truly the case.

(c) The comparisons are factual, accurate and capable of substantiation.
(d) There is no likelihood of the consumer being misled as a result of the comparison, whether about the product advertised or that with which it is compared.
(e) The advertisement does not unfairly denigrate, attack or discredit other products, advertisers or advertisements directly or by implication.

2. Advertisements shall not make unjustifiable use of the name or initials of any other firm, company or institution, nor take unfair advantage of the goodwill attached to the trade mark or symbol of another firm or its product or the goodwill acquired by its advertising campaign.
3. Advertisements shall not be similar to any other advertiser's earlier run advertisements in general layout, copy, slogans, visual presentations, music or sound effects, so as to suggest plagiarism.
4. As regards matters covered by sections 2 and 3 above, complaints of plagiarism of advertisements released earlier abroad will lie outside the scope of this Code except in the under-mentioned circumstances:
   (a) The complaint is lodged within 12 months of the first general circulation of the advertisements/campaign complained against.
   (b) The complainant provides substantiation regarding the claim of prior invention/usage abroad.

Guidelines for Specific Category Advertisements

Self-Regulation Guidelines on Advertisements for Automotive vehicles

Preamble:

Advertisements have a significant influence on people's behaviour. As such, advertisers are encouraged to depict advertisements, in a manner which promotes safe practices, e.g. wearing of helmets and fastening of seat belts, not using mobiles/cell phones when driving, etc.

Guidelines:

Specifically, advertisements should not:

a) Portray violation of the Traffic Rules,
b) Show speed manoeuvrability in a manner which encourages unsafe or reckless driving, which could harm the driver, passengers and/or general public,

c) Show stunts or actions, which require professional driving skills, in normal traffic conditions which in any case should carry a readable cautionary message drawing viewer attention to the depiction of stunts.

Guidelines for Qualification of Brand Extension Product or Service

In order to evaluate the genuineness of an unrestricted product or service brand extension of a product (e.g. liquor and tobacco) whose advertising is prohibited by law, 'The Advertising Standards Council of India' (ASCI) has decided the following objective criteria to be used to qualify a correct Brand Extension product or service (see Chapter III Clause 3.6 (a) of ASCI code)

1. Brand Extension Product or Service should be registered with appropriate government authority e.g. CENVAT/ VAT/FDA/FSSAI/ TM etc.
2. (a) In store availability of the product must be at least 10% of the leading brand in the category the product competes as measured in the metro cities where the product is advertised.
   OR
2. (b) Sales Turnover of the product or service on should exceed Rs.5 cr per annum nationally or Rs 1 cr per annum per state where distribution has been established.
3. A valid certificate from an independent organization such as 'ACNielsen' or category 'Specific Industry Association' (for distribution and sales turnover) would be required to prove the concerned criteria.

Self-Regulation Guidelines on Advertising of Foods & Beverages (F&B)

Preamble:

Communication and advertisements related to F&B can have significant impact on the lives of the public in general and their physical and material well being in particular. It is, therefore, imperative that F&B advertisements fulfil their intended roles and advertisers adopt strict principles of self-regulation and not mislead the general public in any manner detrimental to well being. Caution and care should be observed in advertising of F&B, especially, ones containing relatively high fat, sugar and salt (HFSS).

Recognizing the need to promote high standards of business ethics to ensure commercial communication to consumers are responsible and the need to provide honest and truthful information about food and beverage products are met, the following guidelines are issued.

Guidelines:

1) Advertisements should not be misleading or deceptive. Specifically, advertisements should not mislead consumers to believe that consumption of product advertised will result directly in personal changes in intelligence, physical ability or exceptional recognition. Such claims if made in advertisements should be supported and substantiated with evidence and with adequate scientific basis.
2) Advertisements that include what consumer, acting reasonably, might interpret as health or nutritional claims shall be supported by appropriate scientific evidence and meeting the requirement of basic food standards laid down under the Food Safety Standards Act and Rules, wherever applicable.
3) Advertisements should not disparage good dietary practice or the selection of options, such as fresh fruits and vegetables that accepted dietary opinion recommends should form part of the normal diet.
4) Advertisements should not encourage over or excessive consumption or show inappropriately large portions of any food or beverage. It should reflect moderation in consumption and show portion sizes appropriate to the occasion or situation.
5) Advertisements should also not undermine the importance of healthy lifestyles or mislead as to the nutritive value of the food or beverage.
6) Advertisement should not undermine the role of parental care and guidance in ensuring proper food choices are made by children.
7) Advertisements for food or beverages unless nutritionally designed as such should not be promoted or portrayed as a meal replacement.
8) Claims in advertisements should not be inconsistent with information on the label or packaging of the food or beverage.
9) Advertisement for food and beverages should not claim or imply endorsement by any government agency, professional body, independent agency or individual in a particular profession in India; unless, there is a prior consent, the claim is current and endorsement verifiable and agency body named.

Guidelines for Advertising of Educational Institutions and Programs

Preamble:

Educational Institutions such as Universities, colleges, schools, coaching classes etc., which offer programs of education and training play a vital role in building the intellectual capital of India. Parents place a very high value on the education of their children and are known to make great personal sacrifices to enable their children to get the right education. Unlike a tangible product where it is frequently possible to judge the value of what is being offered by inspection and demonstration, in the field of education and training the value of a program is judged mainly by means such as degrees, diplomas and other qualification nomenclatures, recognition, affiliations, testimonials, accreditations, admissions/job/compensation promises – of which the variety being advertised are many. A significant amount of advertising activity is currently happening reflecting the vast variety of educational programs which are being offered. Guidelines, further to complying with the general rules of ASCI's Code for Self - Regulation in Advertising, the advertisements of Educational Institutions and Programs shall comply with the following

Guidelines:

1. The advertisement shall not state or lead the public to believe that an institution or course or program is official, recognized, authorized, accredited, approved, registered, affiliated, endorsed or has a legal defined situation, unless the advertiser is able to substantiate with evidence.

2.(a) An advertisement offering a degree or diploma or certificate which by law requires to be recognized or approved by an authority shall have the name of that authority specified for that particular field.

2.(b) In case the advertised institution or program is not recognized or approved by any mandatory authority, but is affiliated to another institution, which is approved or recognized by a mandatory authority, then the full name and location of the said affiliating institution shall also be stated in the advertisement.

2.(c) The name of the affiliating institution, as indicated in 2(b), shall not be less than 50% of the font size as that of the advertised institution or program in visual media such as print, internet, hoarding, leaflet, prospectus etc., including television. In audio media such as radio or TV the name of the affiliating institution (if applicable), must be stated.

3. Advertisement shall not state or lead the public to believe that enrolment in the institution or program or preparation course or coaching classes will provide the student a temporary or permanent job, admissions to institutions, job promotions, salary increase etc. unless the advertiser is able to submit substantiation to such effect. In addition, the advertisement must carry a disclaimer stating 'Past record is no guarantee of future job prospects.' The font size of the disclaimer should not be less than the size of the claim being made in the advertisements.

4. (a) Advertisement shall not make claims regarding extent of the passing batch placed, highest or average compensation of the students placed, enrolment of students, admissions of students to renowned educational institutes, marks and ranking of students passed out, testimonial of topper students, institution's or its program's competitive ranking, size and qualification of its faculty, affiliation with a foreign institution, institute's infrastructure, etc. unless they are of the latest completed academic year and substantiated with evidence.

4.(b) Advertisement stating competitive rank of the institution or its program shall also provide full name and date of the publication or medium which released the rankings.

4.(c) Visual of infrastructure of the institution shown in advertisement shall be real and existing at the time of advertisement's release.

4.(d) Testimonial of toppers in an advertisement shall be from students who have participated in the testimony program, exams or subject only from the advertising institute.

4.(e) An advertisement stating the number of passing out students placed for jobs shall also state total number of students passing out from the placed class.

ASCI's policy on complaints against Political and Government advertisements

ASCI does not accept and process complaints against political and non-commercial government advertising for the following reasons:

1) ASCI's self-regulation system is established as an industry initiative with the objective of regulating commercial communication, i.e. advertising which, directly or indirectly, solicits the exchange of money for goods and services. ASCI's code specifically states that "The code for self- regulation has been accepted by individuals, corporate bodies

and associations engaged in or otherwise concerned with the practice of advertising in the best interest of the ultimate consumer." Therefore, political, and non-commercial government advertising attempting to influence voters does not come under the ambit of ASCI.

2) It is important to ASCI's integrity that it is seen as an impartial adjudicator free from the perception of political bias. It is not possible to make decisions about whether a political or non-commercial government advertisement breaches the Code without the potential for being seen as taking a political viewpoint.
3) ASCI has mandates from industry associations such as ISA, AAAI, INS, IBF, etc. representing India's advertisers, advertising agencies and media to self-regulate advertising content. ASCI currently has no mandate to regulate government or political advertising. Complainants need to be aware that the ASCI is an industry funded body. It is inappropriate for ASCI to assume jurisdiction over the content of political or government advertising in the absence of political parties' or government's support for such advertising to be regulated by ASCI. ASCI recommends that anyone who has complaints against any political advertisements should write to the Election Commission of India. And send complaints against non-commercial government- released TV advertisements to Ministry of Information and Broadcasting, New Delhi, which is the regulator for TV content and for press advertisements to the Press Council of India, New Delhi which is the regulator for print content.

ASCI's Minimum lettering Size and Duration requirement of "Supers" communicating Disclaimers, Qualifications, etc. in an Advertisement

'Supers' should be clearly legible and on TV advertisements should be held long enough for the full message to be read by an average viewer on a standard domestic TV set. Therefore, following minimum size of the lettering of 'Supers' and its holding time on screen for the TV advertisements is required.

1) For print advertisements the font size of the 'Supers' shall be minimum 6 and 7 points for 100 column centimeters or less and more than 100 column centimeters or equivalent size advertisements respectively.
2) For TV advertisements the size of the 'Supers' shall be of minimum 12 pixel height and stay not less than 4 seconds duration on the screen for upto 2 lines of 'Supers'. For every additional line of 'Super' additional 2

seconds of hold time would be required. Script of the 'Supers' should be in the same language as the audio of the advertisement.

Guidelines of Advertising for Skin Lightening or Fairness Improvement Products

Preamble:

While all fairness products are licensed for manufacture and sale by the relevant state Food & Drug Administrations (FDA) under the Drugs & Cosmetics Act, there is a strong concern in certain sections of society that advertising of fairness products tends to communicate and perpetuate the notion that dark skin is inferior and undesirable. ASCI code's Chapter III 1(b) already states that advertisements should not deride race, caste, colour, creed or nationality. Yet, given how widespread the advertising for fairness and skin lightening products is and the concerns of different stakeholders in society, ASCI therefore felt a need to frame specific guidelines for this product category.

Guidelines:

The following guidelines are to be used when creating and assessing advertisements in this category.

1) Advertising should not communicate any discrimination as a result of skin colour. These ads should not reinforce negative social stereotyping on the basis of skin colour. Specifically, advertising should not directly or implicitly show people with darker skin, in a way which is widely seen as, unattractive, unhappy, depressed or concerned. These ads should not portray people with darker skin, in a way which is widely seen as, at a disadvantage of any kind, or inferior, or unsuccessful in any aspect of life, particularly in relation to being attractive to the opposite sex, matrimony, job placement, promotions and other prospects.
2) In the pre-usage depiction of product, special care should be taken to ensure that the expression of the model/s in the real and graphical representation should not be negative in a way which is widely seen as unattractive, unhappy, depressed or concerned.
3) Advertising should not associate darker or lighter colour skin with any particular socio-economic strata, caste, community, religion, profession or ethnicity.
4) Advertising should not perpetuate gender based discrimination because of skin colour.

ANNEXURE II

Details of IPC Sections 153A, 295 & 295A

Section 153 A:

The purpose of the Section 153 A is to punish persons who indulge in wanton vilification or attacks upon the religion, race, place of birth, residence, language etc of any particular group or class or upon the founders and prophets of a religion. The jurisdiction of this Section is widened so as to make promotion of disharmony, enmity or feelings of hatred or ill-will between different religious, racial, language or regional groups or castes or communities punishable. Offence on moral turpitude is also covered in this section.

The offence is a cognizable offence and the punishment for the same may extend to three years, or with fine, or with both. However, the punishment of the offence committed in a place of worship is enhanced up to five years and fine.

Ingredients of Section 153A:

- The act of promoting enmity between different groups on grounds of religion, race, place of birth, residence, language, caste, community or any other group.
- Acts prejudicial to the maintenance of harmony between different groups or castes or communities, if the acts disturb public tranquility.
- Acts causing fear or alarm or a feeling of insecurity among members of any religious, racial, language or regional group or caste or community by use of criminal force or violence against them.

Section 295:

Section 295 of the I.P.C makes destruction, damage, or defilement of a place of worship or an object held sacred, with intent to insult the religion of a class of persons, punishable with imprisonment which may extend to two years, or with fine , or with both. This section has been enacted to compel people to respect the religious susceptibilities of persons of different religious persuasion or creeds.

Ingredients of Section 295:

- The accused must do such an act with the intention of insulting the religion of any person, or with the knowledge that any class of person is likely to consider such destruction, damage or defilement as an insult to their religion.
- The accused must destroy , damage or defile any place of worship or any object which is held as sacred by any class of persons.

Section 295-A:

The object of Section 295-A is to punish deliberate and malicious acts intended to outrage the religious feelings of any class by insulating its religion or the religious beliefs. This section only punishes an aggravated form of insult to religion when it is perpetrated with deliberate and malicious intention of outraging the religious feelings of a class.

Ingredients of Section 295-A:

- The accused must insult or attempt to insult the religion or religious beliefs of any class of citizens of India.
- The said insult must be with a deliberate and malicious intention of outraging the religious feelings of the said class of citizens.
- The said insult must be by words, either spoken or written, by signs or by visible representation or otherwise.
- The offence under Section 295-A is cognizable and a non-bailable and non-compoundable offence.
- The police have a power under to arrest a person charged under Section 295-A without a warrant.

ANNEXURE III

Programme and Advertising Codes Prescribed under the Cable Television Network Rules, 1994 (Rule 6 and Rule 7)

Rule- 6. Programme Code

(1) No programme should be carried in the cable service which:-

(a) Offends against good taste or decency;

(b) Contains criticism of friendly countries;

(c) Contains attack on religions or communities or visuals or words contemptuous of religious groups or which promote communal attitudes;

(d) Contains anything obscene, defamatory, deliberate, false and suggestive innuendos and half truths;

(e) is likely to encourage or incite violence or contains anything against maintenance of law and order or which promote anti-national attitudes;

(f) Contains anything amounting to contempt of court;

(g) Contains aspersions against the integrity of the President and Judiciary;

(h) Contains anything affecting the integrity of the Nation;

(i) Criticises, maligns or slanders any individual in person or certain groups, segments of social, public and moral life of the country ;

(j) Encourages superstition or blind belief;

(k) Denigrates women through the depiction in any manner of the figure of a women, her form or body or any part thereof in such a way as to have the effect of being indecent, or derogatory to women, or is likely to deprave, corrupt or injure the public morality or morals;

(l) Denigrates children;

(m) Contains visuals or words which reflect a slandering, ironical and snobbish attitude in the portrayal of certain ethnic, linguistic and regional groups ;

(n) Contravenes the provisions of the Cinematograph Act, 1952.

(o) is not suitable for unrestricted public exhibition.

"Provided that no film or film song or film promo or film trailer or music video or music albums or their promos, whether produced in India or abroad, shall be carried through cable service unless it has been certified by the Central Board of Film Certification (CBFC) as suitable for unrestricted public exhibition in India".

Explanation - For the purpose of this clause, the expression "unrestricted public exhibition" shall have the same meaning as assigned to it in the Cinematograph Act, 1952 (37 of 1952);

(2) The cable operator should strive to carry programmes in his cable service which project women in a positive, leadership role of sobriety, moral and character building qualities.

(3) No cable operator shall carry or include in his cable service any programme in respect of which copyright subsists under the Copyright Act, 1957 (14 of 1957) unless he has been granted a licence by owners of copyright under the Act in respect of such programme.

(4) Care should be taken to ensure that programmes meant for children do not contain any bad language or explicit scenes of violence.

(5) Programmes unsuitable for children must not be carried in the cable service at times when the largest numbers of children are viewing.

(6) No cable operator shall carry or include in his cable service any television broadcast or channel, which has not been registered by the Central Government for being viewed within the territory of India".

"Provided that a cable operator may continue to carry or include in his cable service any Television broadcast or channel, whose application for registration to the Central Government was made on or before 11th May, 2006 and is under consideration, for a period of three months from the date of this notification, or till such registration has been granted or refused, whichever is earlier."

"Provided further that channels uplinking from India, in accordance with permission for uplinking granted before 2nd December, 2005, shall be treated as "registered" television channels and can be carried or included in the cable service."

Rule-7. Advertising Code

(1) Advertising carried in the cable service shall be so designed as to conform to the laws of the country and should not offend morality, decency and religious susceptibilities of the subscribers.

(2) No advertisement shall be permitted which-

(i) derides any race, caste, colour, creed and nationality;
(ii) is against any provision of the Constitution of India.
(iii) tends to incite people to crime, cause disorder or violence or breach of law or glorifies violence or obscenity in any way ;
(iv) presents criminality as desirable;
(v) exploits the national emblem, or any part of the Constitution or the person or personality of a national leader or a State dignitary;
(vi) in its depiction of women violates the constitutional guarantees to all citizens. In particular, no advertisement shall be permitted which projects a derogatory image of women. Women must not be portrayed in a manner that emphasises passive, submissive qualities and encourages them to play a subordinate, secondary role in the family and society. The cable operator shall ensure that the portrayal of the female form, in the programmes carried in his cable service, is tasteful and aesthetic, and is within the well established norms of good taste and decency;
(vii) exploits social evils like dowry, child marriage.
(viii) promotes directly or indirectly production, sale or consumption of-

(A) cigarettes, tobacco products, wine, alcohol, liquor or other intoxicants; provided that a product that uses a brand name or logo, which is also used for cigarettes, tobacco products, wine, alcohol, liquor or other intoxicants, may be advertised on cable service subject to the following conditions that:-

(i the story board or visual of the advertisement must depict only the product being advertised and not the prohibited products in any form or manner;
(ii) the advertisement must not make any direct or indirect reference to the prohibited products;
(iii) the advertisement must not contain any nuances or phrases promoting prohibited products;
(iv) the advertisement must not use particular colours and layout or presentations associated with prohibited products;
(v) the advertisement must not use situations typical for promotion of prohibited products when advertising the other products;

Provided further that-

(i) the advertiser shall submit an application with a copy of the proposed advertisement along with a certificate by a registered Chartered Accountant that the product carrying the same name as cigarettes, tobacco products, wine, alcohol, liquor or other intoxicants is distributed in reasonable quantity and is available in substantial number of outlets where other products of the same category are available and the proposed expenditure on such advertising thereon shall not be disproportionate to the actual sales turnover of the product.

(ii) All such advertisements found to be genuine brand extensions by the Ministry of Information and Broadcasting shall be previewed and certified by the Central Board of Film Certification as suitable for unrestricted public exhibition and are in accordance with the provisions contained in sub-clause (i) to (v) of the first proviso, prior to their telecast or transmission or retransmission.

(B) infant milk substitutes, feeding bottle or infant food.

(3) No advertisement shall be permitted, the objects whereof, are wholly or mainly of a religious or political nature; advertisements must not be directed towards any religious or political end.

(3A) No advertisement shall contain references which hurt religious sentiments.

(4) The goods or services advertised shall not suffer from any defect or deficiency as mentioned in Consumer Protection Act, 1986.

(5) No advertisement shall contain references which are likely to lead the public to infer that the product advertised or any of its ingredients has some special or miraculous or super-natural property or quality, which is difficult of being proved.

(6) The picture and the audible matter of the advertisement shall not be excessively 'loud;

(7) No advertisement which endangers the safety of children or creates in them any interest in unhealthy practices or shows them begging or in an undignified or indecent manner shall not be carried in the cable service.

(8) Indecent, vulgar, suggestive, repulsive or offensive themes or treatment shall be avoided in all advertisements.

(9) No advertisement which violates the Code for self-regulation in advertising, as adopted by the Advertising Standard Council

of India (ASCI), Mumbai, for public exhibition in India, from time to time, shall be carried in the cable service.

(10) All advertisement should be clearly distinguishable from the programme and should not in any manner interfere with the programme viz., use of lower part of screen to carry captions, static or moving alongside the programme.

(11) No programme shall carry advertisements exceeding twelve minutes per hours, which may include up to ten minutes per hour of commercial advertisements, and up to two minutes per hour of the channel's self-promotional programmes.

ANNEXURE IV

List of Laws, Rules and Regulations that Deal with Advertisements

The major rules, regulations and legislations include:

- Constitution of India;
- Indian Penal Code, 1860;
- The Contract Act, 1872;
- The Drugs and Cosmetics Act, 1940;
- The Emblems and Names (Prevention of Improper Use) Act, 1950;
- The Drugs and Magic Remedies (Objectionable Advertisements) Act, 1955;
- The Young Persons (Harmful Publications) Act, 1956;
- The Civil Defense Act, 1968
- The Cigarettes (Regulation of Production, Supply and Distribution) Act, 1975;
- Consumer Protection Act, 1986;
- Indecent Representation of Women (Prohibition) Act, 1986;
- Securities and Exchange Board of India (SEBI) (Stock-brokers and Sub-brokers) Rules, 1992;
- The Infant Milk Substitutes, Feeding Bottles and Infant Foods (Regulation of Production, Supply and Distribution) Act, 1992;
- The Prenatal Diagnostic Techniques (Regulation and Prevention of Misuse) Act, 1994;
- The Transplantation of Human Organs Act, 1994;
- Code of Conduct for Stock-brokers, Securities and Exchange Board of India (SEBI) (Prohibition of Fraudulent and Unfair Trade Practices relating to Securities Market) Regulations, 1995;
- Securities and Exchange Board of India (SEBI) (Mutual Funds Regulation), 1996;
- The Representation of the People (Amendment) Act, 1996;
- The Lotteries (Regulation) Act, 1998;

- Information Technology Act, 2000;
- SEBI Guidelines for Advertisements by Mutual Funds, Securities and Exchange Board of India (SEBI) (Disclosure and Investor Protection Guidelines), 2000;
- The Competition Act, 2002;
- The Cigarettes and other Tobacco Products (Prohibition of Advertisement and Regulation of Trade and Commerce, Production, Supply and Distribution) Act, 2003 and
- Advertising Standards Council of India (ASCI) among others.

Bibliography

Books

Aggarwal, V. B., & Gupta, V. S. (2001). *Handbook of journalism and mass communication*. New Delhi: Concept Publishing Company.

Awasthi, S. K., Kataria, R. P., & Orient Publishing Company. (2006). *Law relating to protection of human rights*. New Delhi: Orient Pub. Co.

Bajpai, A. (2003). *Child rights in India: Law, policy, and practice*. New Delhi: Oxford University Press.

Basu, D. D. (1971). *Introduction to the Constitution of India*. Calcutta: S.C. Sarkar.

Blocher, H. (2003). *Advertising Ethics - An Oxymoron?* New Castle Business School, New Castle.

Bootwala, S., Lawrence, M. D., & Mali, S. R. (2007). *Advertising and sales promotion*. Pune: Nirali Prakashan.

Cacioppo, J. T., & Freberg, L. (2013). *Discovering psychology: The science of mind*. Belmont, CA: Wadsworth Cengage Wadsworth.

Ciochetto, L. (2013). *Globalisation and advertising in emerging economies: Brazil, Russia, India and China*. Routledge.

Crompton, J. L., & Lamb, C. W. (1986). *Marketing government and social services*. New York: Wiley.

Douglas, T. (1986). *The complete guide to advertising*. Papermac.

Gupta, O. (2005). *Advertising in India: Trends and impact*. Delhi: Kalpaz Publications.

Ingham, J. N. (1983). *Biographical dictionary of American business leaders: [1]*. Westport, CT: Greenwood Press.

Jain, A. (2009). *Principles of marketing*. VK Publications.

Kaptan, S. S. (2002). *Advertising, new concepts*. New Delhi: Sarup & Sons.

Kazmi, S. H., & Batra, S. K. (2008). *Advertising & sales promotion*. New Delhi: Excel Books.

Kitchlu, T. N. (1996). *Exploited child: A national problem*. New Delhi: M D Publications.

Macklin, M. C., & Carlson, L. (1999). *Advertising to Children: Concepts and Controversies*. Sage Publications.

Mandell, M. I. (1974). *Advertising*. Englewood Cliffs, NJ: Prentice-Hall.

McDonough, J., & Egolf, K. (2015). *The Advertising age encyclopedia of advertising*. Routledge.

Medoff, N. J., & Kaye, B. K. (2010). *Electronic media: Then, now, and later*. Taylor & Francis.

Pathak, J. P. (2014). *Introduction to media laws and ethics*. Delhi: Shipra Publications.

Schaffter, S. J. (2006). *Privileging the privileged: Gender in Indian advertising*. New Delhi: Promilla & Co., Publishers, in association with Bibliophile South Asia.

Schultz, E. A., & Lavenda, R. H. (2005). *Cultural anthropology: A perspective on the human condition*. New York: Oxford University Press.

Shah, K. (2014). *Advertising and integrated marketing communicatons*. New Delhi: McGraw Hill Education (India.

Shah, K., & D'Souza, A. (2009). *Advertising & Promotions*. Tata McGraw-Hill Education.

Sharma, S., & Singh, R. (2006). *Advertising: Planning and Implementation*. PHI Learning Pvt. Ltd.

Singh, M. P. (2007). *Quote Unquote A Handbook of Famous Quotations*. Lotus Books.

Trehan, M., & Trehan, R. (2007). *Advertising and sales management*. FK Publications.

United States. (2002). *The Optional Protocol to the Convention on the Rights of the Child on the Sale of Children, Child Prostitution and Child Pornography and the Optional Protocol to the Convention on the Rights of the Child on the Involvement of Children in Armed Conflict: Report (to accompany Treaty doc. 106-37)*. Washington, D.C.: U.S. G.P.O.

Usman, M. (2014). An evaluation of ethics in television advertising in India: a case study of Bangalore district, University of Mysore.

Vadehra, S. (2004). Advertising to Children in India. *World Advertising Research Center 2004, Young Consumers, 4*, 113-131.

Van, B. G. (1995). *The international law on the rights of the child*. Dordrecht: M. Nijhoff.

Venkateswaran, K. S., & Asian Mass Communication Research and Information Centre. (1993). *Mass media laws and regulations in India*.

Journals

Aaker, D. A., & Bruzzone, D. E. (1985). Causes of Irritation in Advertising. *Journal of Marketing, 49*(2), 47. doi:10.2307/1251564

Appiah, O. (2001). Ethnic Identification on Adolescents' Evaluations of Advertisements. *Journal of Advertising Research, 41*(5), 7-22. doi:10.2501/jar-41-5-7-22

Arrington, R. L. (1982). Advertising and behavior control. *Journal of Business Ethics, 1*(1), 3-12. doi:10.1007/bf00382800

Berger, I. E., & Mitchell, A. A. (1989). The Effect of Advertising on Attitude Accessibility, Attitude Confidence, and the Attitude-Behavior Relationship. *Journal of Consumer Research, 16*(3), 269. doi:10.1086/209213

Browne, B. A. (1998). Gender Stereotypes in Advertising on Children's Television in the 1990s: A Cross-National Analysis. *Journal of Advertising, 27*(1), 83-96. doi:10.1080/00913367.1998.10673544

Burkhart, G. (2003). Same-Sex Love in India: Readings from Literature and History. Edited by Ruth Vanita and Saleem Kidwai. New York: St. Martin's Press, 2000. 352 pp. $55.00 (cloth). *The Journal of Asian Studies, 62*(01), 322-323. doi:10.2307/3096220

Ciochetto, L. (2004). Advertising and Globalization in India. *Media Asia, 31*(3), 157-169. doi:10.1080/01296612.2004.11726750

Coltrane, S., & Messineo, M. (2000). The Perpetuation of Subtle Prejudice: Race and Gender Imagery in 1990s Television Advertising. *Sex Roles, 42*(5/6), 363-389. doi:10.1023/a:1007046204478

Das, M. (2010). Gender Role Portrayals in Indian Television Ads. *Sex Roles, 64*(3-4), 208-222. doi:10.1007/s11199-010-9750-1

Drumwright, M. E., & Murphy, P. E. (2004). The Current State of Advertising Ethics. *Journal of Advertising, 38*(1), 83-107.

Fay, M., & Price, C. (1994). Female Body-shape in Print Advertisements and the Increase in Anorexia Nervosa. *European Journal of Marketing, 28*(12), 5-18. doi:10.1108/03090569410074246

Foley, J. P. (1999). Misplaced marketing commentary. *Journal of Consumer Marketing, 16*(3), 220-223. doi:10.1108/07363769910271450

Haefner, M. J. (1991). Ethical Problems of Advertising to Children. *Journal of Mass Media Ethics, 6*(2), 83-92. doi:10.1207/s15327728jmme0602_2

Hyman, M. R., Tansey, R., & Clark, J. W. (1994). Research on Advertising Ethics: Past, Present, and Future. *Journal of Advertising, 23*(3), 5-15. doi:10.1080/00913367.1994.10673446

Jobber, D. (1974). Television advertising: a consumer viewpoint. *European Journal of Marketing, 8*(2), 158-167. doi:10.1108/eum0000000005084

Latour, M. S., & Henthorne, T. L. (1994). Ethical Judgments of Sexual Appeals in Print Advertising. *Journal of Advertising, 23*(3), 81-90. doi:10.1080/00913367.1994.10673453

Lavine, H., Sweeney, D., & Wagner, S. H. (1999). Depicting Women as Sex Objects in Television Advertising: Effects on Body Dissatisfaction. *Personality and Social Psychology Bulletin, 25*(8), 1049-1058. doi:10.1177/01461672992511012

Mittal, M., Daga, A., Chhabra, G., & Lilani, J. (2010). Parental Perception of the Impact of Television Advertisements on Children's Buying Behavior. *The IUP Journal of Marketing Management, 9*(1), 40-54.

Munshi, S. (1998). Wife/mother/daughter-in-law: multiple avatars of homemaker in 1990s Indian advertising. *Media, Culture & Society, 20*(4), 573-591. doi:10.1177/016344398020004004

Pathak, J. P. (2014). Advertisements through unclad babies vis-à-vis their Child Rights. *IOSR Journal of Humanities and Social Science, 19*(11), 08-17. doi:10.9790/0837-191160817

Pathak, J. P. (2014). Portrayal of child delivery in Indian Tv Advertisements vis-à-vis Right to Privacy of Women. *IOSR Journal of Humanities and Social Science, 19*(5), 06-14. doi:10.9790/0837-19530614

Pathak, J. P. (2015). Portrayal of Lasciviousness; an Analysis of Indian TV Ads. Retrieved from http://iosrjournals.org/iosr-jhss/papers/Vol20-issue4/Version-6/C020462028.pdf

Pathak, J. P. (2016). Portrayal of communal harmony: An analysis of Indian TV Ads. Retrieved from www.questjournals.org/jrhss/papers/vol4-issue7/F475057.pdf

Patidar, B., & Gupta, D. (2013). Ethical values in advertisement and Indian society. *EXCEL International Journal of Multidisciplinary Management Studies, 3*(2), 280-284.

Pollay, R. W. (2000). The Distorted Mirror: Reflections on the Unintended Consequences of Advertising. *Advertising & Society Review, 1*(1). doi:10.1353/asr.2000.0012

Richins, M. L. (1991). Social Comparison and the Idealized Images of Advertising. *J CONSUM RES, 18*(1), 71. doi:10.1086/209242

Sengupta, S., & Frith, K. T. (1997). Multinational corporation advertising and cultural imperialism: A content analysis of Indian television commercials. *Asian Journal of Communication, 7*(1), 1-18. doi:10.1080/01292989709388295

Sharma, A. (2012). Portrayal of women in mass media. *Media Watch: An International Journal in Media and Communication.*

Srikandath, S. (1991). Cultural values depicted in Indian television advertising. *International Communication Gazette, 48*(3), 165-176. doi:10.1177/001654929104800302

Tai, H. S. (1999). Advertising Ethics: The Use of Sexual Appeal in Chinese Advertising. *Teaching Business Ethics, 3*(1), 87-100. doi:10.1023/a:1009840623567

Taylor, C. R., & Stern, B. B. (1997). Asian-Americans: Television Advertising and the "Model Minority" Stereotype. *Journal of Advertising, 26*(2), 47-61. doi:10.1080/00913367.1997.10673522

Vyas, D. (2013). CONSUMER UNDERSTANDING FOR ADVERTISING ETHICS: AN EMPIRICAL ANALYSIS. *International Journal of Applied Services Marketing Perspectives, 2*(3), 481-484.

Waller, D. S. (1999). Attitudes towards offensive advertising: an Australian study. *Journal of Consumer Marketing, 16*(3), 288-295. doi:10.1108/07363769910271513

Whittler, T. E. (1991). The Effects of Actors' Race in Commercial Advertising: Review and Extension. *Journal of Advertising, 20*(1), 54-60. doi:10.1080/00913367.1991.10673207

Websites

1. *11 Indian Brands Support The LGBT Community On Facebook Amidst SC's #Sec377 Ruling | Lighthouse Insights.* (n.d.). Retrieved from http://lighthouseinsights.in/11-indian-brands-support-the-lgbt-community-on-facebook-amidst-scs-sec377-ruling.html/
2. *15 Indian Print & Television Advertisements That Courted Controversy.* (n.d.). Retrieved from https://www.scoopwhoop.com/inothernews/indian-advertisements-controversies/#.1r4jscxkn
3. *99 ngos are fraud money-making devices: HC.* (n.d.). Retrieved from http://www.hindustantimes.com/india-news/newdelhi/99-ngos-are-fraud-money-making-devices-hc/article1-1021701.aspx
4. *The Advertisements that almost said it 'All'.* (n.d.). Retrieved from http://english.kolkata24x7.com/lifestyle/the-advertisements-that-almost-said-it-all
5. *Advertising & Child.* (n.d.). Retrieved from http://shodhganga.inflibnet.ac.in/bitstream/10603/92565/10/10_chapter2.pdf
6. *Advertising & Marketing Industry News - AdAge.* (n.d.). Retrieved from http://www.adageindia.in/advertising/harvey-b-brown-creates-jabongs-new-campaign/articleshow/52556240.cms
7. *The Advertising Standards Council of India.* (n.d.). Retrieved from http://www.ascionline.org/images/pdf/asci_code_new.pdf
8. Advertising, Marketing, Media, Digital, PR News & more | Campaign India. (n.d.). Retrieved from http://www.campaignindia.in
9. *After Hindu-Muslim Neighbor Ad, Red Label Tea Touches Upon Live-in Relationships In New Ad | Lighthouse Insights.* (n.d.). Retrieved from http://lighthouseinsights.in/red-label-tea-ive-in-relationships-ad-new-ad.html/
10. Agarwal, A. (1995, March 31). Battling for the big bucks. Retrieved from http://indiatoday.intoday.in/story/despite-competition-from-private-channels-doordarshan-survives-eyes-increase-in-revenues/1/288511.html
11. *Airtel breaks barriers to break the clutter.* (n.d.). Retrieved from http://www.afaqs.com/news/story/20051_Airtel-breaks-barriers-to-break-the-clutter
12. *Ambuja Cement builds awareness, urges India to break invisible walls of divisiveness | Advertising | Campaign India.* (n.d.). Retrieved from http://www.campaignindia.in/video/ambuja-cement-builds-awareness-urges-india-to-break-invisible-walls-of-divisiven/420647
13. *Amour - A dating platform for Queer.* (n.d.). Retrieved from http://amourqueerdating.blogspot.in/
14. *Amour - A Brand New Dating Platform For Queer Indians. – GayIndia.* (n.d.). Retrieved from https://gayrightsindia.wordpress.com/2016/07/21/amour-a-brand-new-dating-platform-for-queer-indians/
15. *annavetticadgoes2themovies: Stars who endorse fainess products/Article published in the new Indian Express.* (n.d.). Retrieved from http://annavetticadgoes2themovies.blogspot.in/2015/04/stars-who-endorse-fairness-products.html

16. *Anouk's ad featuring a lesbian couple has a powerful message for India | Latest News & Updates at Daily News & Analysis.* (n.d.). Retrieved from http://www.dnaindia.com/lifestyle/video-anouk-s-ad-featuring-a-lesbian-couple-has-a-powerful-message-for-india-2094505
17. *Anouk's ad featuring a lesbian couple has a powerful message for India - GenX i Social Buzz.* (n.d.). Retrieved from http://www.genxisocialbuzz.com/index.php/anouks-ad-featuring-a-lesbian-couple-has-a-powerful-message-for-india/
18. *ASCI to rein in ads featuring skin lightening products - The Hindu.* (n.d.). Retrieved from http://www.thehindu.com/business/Industry/asci-to-rein-in-ads-featuring-skin-lightening-products/article6104818.ece
19. Balakrishnan, R., & Bhatt, S. (2014, June 11). *Change in the air in ad world - Fairness Norms Now in Black and White - Mumbai -The Economic Times.* Retrieved from http://epaperbeta.timesofindia.com/Article.aspx?eid=31818&articlexml=CHANGE-IN-THE-AIR-IN-AD-WORLD-Fairness-11062014001083
20. *Banned Commercials or ads in india: Amul Macho Undergarments.* (n.d.). Retrieved from http://bannedcommercialsinindia.blogspot.in/2013/03/AmulMacho.html
21. *BBC Three - Undercover Princes.* (n.d.). Retrieved from http://www.bbc.co.uk/programmes/b00gtkyq
22. *Bigg Boss contestant Sushant Divgikar hopes to sensitise TV viewers to LGBT cause - Times of India.* (n.d.). Retrieved from http://timesofindia.indiatimes.com/tv/news/hindi/Bigg-Boss-contestant-Sushant-Divgikar-hopes-to-sensitise-TV-viewers-to-LGBT-cause/articleshow/43251775.cms
23. *Brands flirt with taboo topics in TV ads - Times of India.* (n.d.). Retrieved from http://timesofindia.indiatimes.com/business/india-business/Brands-flirt-with-taboo-topics-in-TV-ads/articleshow/25337309.cms
24. *Brands That Say, "It's Okay To Be Gay" - Youth Connect.* (n.d.). Retrieved from http://www.youthconnect.in/2013/12/18/brands-that-say-its-okay-to-be-gay/
25. *Breaking Down Walls Of Disparity.* (n.d.). Retrieved from http://www.afaqs.com/news/story/40601_Breaking-Down-Walls-Of-Disparity
26. *Brewing Togetherness.* (n.d.). Retrieved from http://www.afaqs.com/news/story/40559_Brewing-Togetherness
27. *Brooke Bond Red Label's 6-Pack Band: How it became a story worth watching again and again | Best Media Info, News and Analysis on Indian Advertising, Marketing and Media Industry.* (n.d.). Retrieved from http://www.bestmediainfo.com/2016/08/brooke-bond-red-labels-6-pack-band-how-it-became-a-story-worth-watching-again-and-again/
28. *Cadbury 5Star promises to 'cure' seriousness.* (n.d.). Retrieved from http://www.campaignindia.in/video/cadbury-5star-promises-to-cure-seriousness/420293
29. *Celebrate 7 Shades of Love at Kashish Mumbai International Queer Film Festival.* (n.d.). Retrieved from www.dnaindia.com/locality/news-tags/kashish-mumbai-international-queer-film-festival

30. *Celina re-launches pro-gay mag Bombay Dost:News18 Videos.* (n.d.). Retrieved from http://www.news18.com/videos/india/celina-bombay-dost-313986.html
31. *Centre won't rush Sec 377 repeal, says Moily - Rediff.com India News.* (n.d.). Retrieved from http://www.rediff.com/news/report/not-rushing-gay-law-repeal-moily/20090628.htm
32. *Challenging the Ethics of Colorism: The Future Is Bright.* (n.d.). Retrieved from http://www.csrwire.com/blog/posts/1099-challenging-the-ethics-of-colourism-the-future-is-bright
33. *Chapter-1 Introduction.* (n.d.). Retrieved from http://shodhganga.inflibnet.ac.in/bitstream/10603/72959/10/10_chapter%201.pdf
34. Chatterji, S. A. (n.d.). How Advertisements Exploit Women. Retrieved from http://www. gather.com/viewArticle.jsp?articleId=281474976719311
35. *Child Rights and Law: a guidebook for legal interventions.* (n.d.). Retrieved from http://www.childlineindia.org.in/pdf/Law-Manual.pdf
36. CHILDLINE India Foundation - Case Studies. (n.d.). Retrieved from http://www.childlineindia.org.in/1098/b1ecasestudies.htm
37. Childline India Foundation Website. (n.d.). Retrieved from http://www.childlineindia.org.in/1098/1098.htm
38. CHILDLINE India Foundation: Child Protection and rights in India, 1098 Child Support. (n.d.). Retrieved from http://www.childlineindia.org.in/
39. *City prepares for gay pride march [Chennai] | Queer Media Watch: India.* (n.d.). Retrieved from https://qmediawatch.wordpress.com/2009/06/20/city-prepares-for-gay-pride-march-chennai/
40. *Coca-Cola Small World Machines: The Coca-Cola Company.* (n.d.). Retrieved from http://www.coca-colacompany.com/stories/happiness-without-borders
41. *Coca-Cola tries to unite India and Pakistan with interactive vending machines that encourage users in both countries to 'make a friend' | Daily Mail Online.* (n.d.). Retrieved from http://www.dailymail.co.uk/indiahome/indianews/article-2330617/Coca-Cola-tries-unite-India-Pakistan-interactive-vending-machines-encourage-users-countries-make-friend.html
42. *Colorism - definition and synonims of «colorism» in english dictionary.* (n.d.). Retrieved from http://englishdictionary.education/en/colorism
43. *Come 26th March, 2014 - Babies In India Will Be 'Born For The Internet'.* (n.d.). Retrieved from https://www.mtsindia.in/corporate/downloads/Come%2026th%20March,%202014%20-%20Babies%20In%20India%20Will%20Be%20'Born%20For%20The%20Internet'.pdf
44. *CONSTITUTION OF THE PEOPLE'S REPUBLIC OF BANGLADESH.* (n.d.). Retrieved from http://hrlibrary.umn.edu/research/bangladesh-constitution.pdf
45. *Crackdown on gay party in Saharanpur, 13 held - Times of India.* (n.d.). Retrieved from http://timesofindia.indiatimes.com/india/Crackdown-on-gay-party-in-Saharanpur-13-held/articleshow/7175530.cms

46. *The crazy skin-lightening ads that have been banned in India - Digiday.* (n.d.). Retrieved from http://digiday.com/brands/four-ads-wont-see-indian-television-ever/
47. *Creativeland Asia eyes the bigger picture.* (n.d.). Retrieved from http://www.campaignindia.in/article/creativeland-asia-eyes-the-bigger-picture/423199
48. *Don't show bias on basis of skin colour: ASCI to fairness cream brands like HUL, Emami | MxM India.* (n.d.). Retrieved from http://www.mxmindia.com/2014/06/dont-show-bias-on-basis-of-skin-colour-asci-to-fairness-cream-brands-like-hul-emami/
49. *Emotional Google ad a viral hit in India and Pakistan - World - CBC News.* (n.d.). Retrieved from http://www.cbc.ca/news/world/emotional-google-ad-a-viral-hit-in-india-and-pakistan-1.2427935
50. *Fevikwik Todo Nahi Jodo | Ads Watcher.* (n.d.). Retrieved from http://adswatcher.blogspot.in/2015/04/fevikwik-todo-nahi-jodo.html
51. *Fifth Kerala LGBT parade pride held - DNA India.* (n.d.). Retrieved from www.dnaindia.com/india/report-fifth-kerala-lgbt-parade-pride-held-2005667
52. *First gay parade held in India's Gujarat state - Telegraph.* (n.d.). Retrieved from http://www.telegraph.co.uk/news/worldnews/asia/india/10360598/First-gay-parade-held-in-Indias-Gujarat-state.html
53. *Gauri Shinde, the woman behind the Tanishq remarriage ad : India, News - India Today.* (n.d.). Retrieved from http://indiatoday.intoday.in/story/tanishq-reamarriage-ad-gauri-shinde/1/320656.html
54. *Gay activists rejoice over Centre's plan, hold parades - Times of India.* (n.d.). Retrieved from http://timesofindia.indiatimes.com/india/Gay-activists-rejoice-over-Centres-plan-hold-parades/articleshow/4713107.cms
55. *Ghost of Bipasha's Past (Bipasha Basu Topless).* (n.d.). Retrieved from https://www.youtube.com/watch?v=DV_x_DZyVbs
56. *Google's Plan to Win Over Indians—by Making Them Cry - The Atlantic.* (n.d.). Retrieved from http://www.theatlantic.com/international/archive/2013/11/googles-plan-to-win-over-indians-by-making-them-cry/281496/
57. *Guidelines to ensure 'fair' play in advertising - NATIONAL - The Hindu.* (n.d.). Retrieved from http://www.thehindu.com/todays-paper/tp-national/guidelines-to-ensure-fair-play-in-advertising/article6105981.ece
58. *Havells fans: For a change.* (n.d.). Retrieved from http://www.afaqs.com/news/story/36920_Havells-fans-For-a-change
59. *History of advertising - An overview.* (n.d.). Retrieved from http://ietd.inflibnet.ac.in/bitstream/10603/375/7/07_chapter2.pdf
60. *History of Advertising in India.* (n.d.). Retrieved from https://www.scribd.com/presentation/103559102/History-of-Advertising-in-India
61. *Homosexuality: Govt opposes HC verdict in apex court.* (n.d.). Retrieved from http://www.mumbaimirror.com/article/3/2012022320120223141327934d025428/Homosexuality-Govt-opposes-HC-verdict-in-apex-court.html

62. *A huge scam running into crores - NEW DELHI - The Hindu.* (n.d.). Retrieved from http://www.thehindu.com/todays-paper/tp-national/tp-newdelhi/a-huge-scam-running-into-crores/article4330537.ece
63. *In 'zeal for unity', Indian, Pakistani filmmakers to bridge divide | The Indian Express.* (n.d.). Retrieved from http://indianexpress.com/article/entertainment/entertainment-others/in-zeal-for-unity-indian-pakistani-filmmakers-to-bridge-divide/
64. *India has 2.5m gays, government tells supreme court - BBC News.* (n.d.). Retrieved from http://www.bbc.com/news/world-asia-india-17363200
65. *INDIA.* (n.d.). Retrieved from www.state.gov/documents/organization/171754.pdf
66. *Indian Fashion Brand Red Lotus Uses All Transgender Models For New Sari Campaign | Huffington Post.* (n.d.). Retrieved from http://www.huffingtonpost.co.uk/entry/transgender-indian-models_uk_5745cc40e4b02163fae84e38
67. *India's gay prince appears on Oprah show.* (n.d.). Retrieved from http://www.rediff.com/news/2007/oct/26look1.htm
68. *Indo-Pakistani wars and conflicts.* (n.d.). Retrieved from https://en.wikipedia.org/wiki/Indo-Pakistani_wars_and_conflicts01125661661
69. Indo-Pakistani wars and conflicts. (n.d.). Retrieved from https://en.wikipedia.org/wiki/Indo-Pakistani_wars_and_conflicts
70. *Introducing child protection.* (n.d.). Retrieved from http://www.unicef.org/violencestudy/pdf/CP%20Manual%20-%20Stage%201.pdf
71. *It's a great honour to be awarded for book on gender variants: Gopi Shankar - Times of India.* (n.d.). Retrieved from http://timesofindia.indiatimes.com/city/madurai/Its-a-great-honour-to-be-awarded-for-book-on-gender-variants-Gopi-Shankar/articleshow/38769130.cms
72. *Jabong launches 'Be You' campaign.* (n.d.). Retrieved from http://www.exchange4media.com/advertising/jabong-launches-be-you-campaign_57474.html
73. *Jabong's New Ad Celebrates Genderfluidity In All Its Glory.* (n.d.). Retrieved from http://www.feminisminindia.com/.../video-jabongs-new-ad-celebrates-genderfluidity-glory/
74. *Journey of fairness creams' advertising in India - Page2 - The Economic Times.* (n.d.). Retrieved from http://economictimes.indiatimes.com/features/brand-equity/journey-of-fairness-creams-advertising-in-india/articleshow/msid-30997189,curpg-2.cms?from=mdr
75. *Kaustav's Arden: Two recent television ads and 'gay' sites of sexual ambivalence.* (n.d.). Retrieved from http://kaustavsarden.blogspot.in/2010/10/two-recent-television-ads-and-gay-sites.html
76. *KBC: cutting across the divide.* (n.d.). Retrieved from http://www.afaqs.com/news/story/41437_KBC-cutting-across-the-divide
77. *Kohinoor Basmati Rice – When boundaries divide, but taste unites | Best Media Info, News and Analysis on Indian Advertising, Marketing and Media Industry.*

(n.d.). Retrieved from http://www.bestmediainfo.com/2015/08/kohinoor-basmati-rice-when-boundaries-divide-but-taste-unites/

78. *Law Commission of India.* (n.d.). Retrieved from lawcommissionofindia.nic.in/1-50/report42.pdf
79. *Lesbian, gay, bisexual and transgender resource guide for employers - Times of India.* (n.d.). Retrieved from http://timesofindia.indiatimes.com/india/Lesbian-gay-bisexual-and-transgender-resource-guide-for-employers/articleshow/16739968.cms
80. *LGBT film festival kick starts second edition in Mumbai.* (n.d.). Retrieved from www.dnaindia.com/entertainment/report-lgbt-film-festival-kick-starts-second-edition-in-mumbai-1547650
81. *LGBT history of India.* (n.d.). Retrieved from https://en.wikipedia.org/wiki/LGBT_history_of_India
82. *Madurai comes out of the closet - The Hindu.* (n.d.). Retrieved from http://www.thehindu.com/news/cities/Madurai/madurai-comes-out-of-the-closet/article3702689.ece
83. *Maiden rainbow pride walk - The Telegraph - Calcutta (Kolkata).* (n.d.). Retrieved from http://www.telegraphindia.com/1090628/jsp/nation/story_11167322.jsp
84. *Men can pout, dance in ghungroos, be gay; Don't judge: eBay India's new spot.* (n.d.). Retrieved from http://www.afaqs.com/news/story/49092_Men-can-pout-dance-in-ghungroos-be-gay-Dont-judge-eBay-Indias-new-spot
85. *Milestones of All India Radio.* (n.d.). Retrieved from http://allindiaradio.gov.in/profile/milestones/pages/default.aspx
86. *MTS gives birth to an internet baby.* (n.d.). Retrieved from http://www.exchange4media.com/advertising/mts-gives-birth-to-an-internet-baby_54848.html
87. MTS India - MTS MBlaze, MTS CDMA India, MTS MBrowse, MTS CDMA SmartPhone, MTS Android Phones. (n.d.). Retrieved from http://www.mtsindia.in/
88. MTS targets 'net gen' again, with an 'internet baby' | Advertising | Campaign India. (n.d.). Retrieved from http://www.campaignindia.in/video/mts-targets-net-gen-again-with-an-internet-baby/420369
89. *New eBay Ad Shows Gay Couple, Breaks Stereotypes On Gender, Age And Religion.* (n.d.). Retrieved from http://www.youthkiawaaz.com/2016/10/ebay-ad-breaking-stereotypes/
90. *Now, a dating platform for LGBT community.* (n.d.). Retrieved from www.dnaindia.com/mumbai/report-now-a-dating-platform-for-lgbt-community-2236832
91. *Obscenity In Television Advertisements: Do we need more stringent measures of scrutiny than used in films?.* (n.d.). Retrieved from http://www.legalera.in/interviews/item/7082-obscenity-in-television-advertisements-do-we-need-more-stringent-measures-of-scrutiny-than-used-in-films

92. *Press Council of India NORMS OF JOURNALISTIC CONDUCT.* (n.d.). Retrieved from http://presscouncil.nic.in/OldWebsite/NORMS-2010.pdf
93. *Pride walk: LGBT group demands social, economic rights | jaipur | Hindustan Times.* (n.d.). Retrieved from http://www.hindustantimes.com/jaipur/pride-walk-lgbt-group-demands-social-economic-rights/story-cVx2yZzg9Bbz9ubtzho0uJ.html
94. *The prince of cool - Titan Industries - Tata group.* (n.d.). Retrieved from http://www.tata.in/article/inside/v4wVshbcNL8=/TLYVr3YPkMU=
95. *Proud to be Out | Tehelka.* (n.d.). Retrieved from http://www.tehelka.com/2013/08/proud-to-be-out/
96. *Queer films from Pakistan, Iran head for Kashish.* (n.d.). Retrieved from www.dnaindia.com/entertainment/report-queer-films-from-pakistan-iran-head-for-kashish-1834780
97. *Queer India: Gay historians: Ruth Vanita and Saleem Kidwai.* (n.d.). Retrieved from http://queerindia.blogspot.in/2005/03/gay-historians-ruth-vanita-and-saleem.html
98. *Queer Pride march in Kochi - KERALA - The Hindu.* (n.d.). Retrieved from http://www.thehindu.com/todays-paper/tp-national/tp-kerala/queer-pride-march-in-kochi/article6253916.ece
99. *Rainbow Chronicles | The Indian Express.* (n.d.). Retrieved from http://indianexpress.com/article/cities/kolkata/rainbow-chronicles/
100. *Ranbir Kapoor - Pepsi TVC 2010.* (n.d.). Retrieved from https://www.youtube.com/watch?v=IJyMtoENWZ0
101. *Reinventing Bisleri.* (n.d.). Retrieved from http://www.icmrindia.org/free%20resources/casestudies/reinventing-bisleri2.htm
102. *Reunion (advertisement).* (n.d.). Retrieved from https://en.wikipedia.org/wiki/Reunion_(advertisement)
103. *Reunion Google Advert Goes Viral.* (n.d.). Retrieved from www.ashugaur.com/reunion-google-advert-viral/
104. *Sania Mirza and Shoaib Malik indulge in Indo-Pak banter in Nestle EveryDay Ad.* (n.d.). Retrieved from http://www.afaqs.com/news/story/47429_Sania-Mirza-and-Shoaib-Malik-indulge-in-Indo-Pak-banter-in-Nestle-EveryDay-Ad
105. *Some HC judges are becoming terribly ignorant of our Constitution!.* (n.d.). Retrieved from http://www.legallyindia.com/Blogs/some-hc-judges-are-becoming-terribly-ignorant-of-our-constitution
106. Srivastava, A. (n.d.). Advertising History. Retrieved from https://www.scribd.com/doc/21560255/Evaluation-of-indian-Advertising-History
107. *Supreme Court pulls up Centre for flip-flop on homosexuality - Indian Express.* (n.d.). Retrieved from http://www.indianexpress.com/news/supreme-court-pulls-up-centre-for-flipflop-on-homosexuality/917743/?google_editors_picks=true

108. *THE CABLE TELEVISION NETWORKS RULES, 1994.* (n.d.). Retrieved from http://www.wipo.int/edocs/lexdocs/laws/en/in/in079en.pdf
109. *THE GENERALS - 8pm Whisky TV Commercial Ad.* (n.d.). Retrieved from http://www.advertolog.com/radico-khaitan/adverts/the-generals-1156005/
110. *This Kaun Banega Crorepati Ad On Hindu-Muslim Harmony Will Blow Your Mind Away - Youth Connect.* (n.d.). Retrieved from http://www.youthconnect.in/2014/.../kaun-banega-crorepati-ad-on-hindu-muslim-harmony/
111. *Titan Fastrack: Come out of the closet... Move on.* (n.d.). Retrieved from https://www.youtube.com/watch?v=yJe9fEx7u58
112. *Top 5 Sexual and Sensual Indian Ads (WIldstone, KS, Maaza, Amul Macho, Manforce).* (n.d.). Retrieved from https://www.youtube.com/watch?v=DNnEBVn_ZOU
113. *UrbanClap launches campaign addressing LGBTQ issues | Indian Television Dot Com.* (n.d.). Retrieved from http://www.indiantelevision.com/mam/media-and-advertising/ad-campaigns/urbanclap-launches-campaign-addressing-lgbtq-issues-160603
114. *UrbanClap supports Lesbian-Gay-Bisexual-Transgender community in new ad.* (n.d.). Retrieved from http://www.afaqs.com/news/story/48160_UrbanClap-supports-Lesbian-Gay-Bisexual-Transgender-community-in-new-ad
115. *Vanity fair- The New Indian Express.* (n.d.). Retrieved from http://www.newindianexpress.com/magazine/2011/jun/26/vanity-fair-266689.html
116. *Viral video: Google ad connects India-Pak with heartwarming reunion story | Page 11.* (n.d.). Retrieved from http://defence.pk/threads/viral-video-google-ad-connects-india-pak-with-heartwarming-reunion-story.287264/page-11
117. *Virgin Mobile India Think Hatke Funny TV Commercial Ad #1.* (n.d.). Retrieved from https://www.youtube.com/watch?v=5FUIqPPlMd0
118. *Why so serious? Cadbury 5 Star offers the perfect cure in latest ad.* (n.d.). Retrieved from http://www.exchange4media.com/advertising/why-so-serious-cadbury-5-star-offers-the-perfect-cure-in-latest-ad_54675.html
119. *World Overnight: Why Indians and Pakistanis Find This Ad Incredibly Moving.* (n.d.). Retrieved from https://punditfromanotherplanet.com/2013/11/14/world-overnight-why-indians-and-pakistanis-find-this-ad-incredibly-moving/
120. *Worldwide gay rights as a social movement picks up.* (n.d.). Retrieved from www.merinews.com/article/worldwide-gay-rights-as-a-social-movement-picks-up/15914647.shtml
121. *YouTube- AC Black - Kuch Bhi Ho Sakta Hai.mp4.* (n.d.). Retrieved from https://www.youtube.com/watch?v=XBd_n_VO8Nc

Index